QUILTS! QUILTS!!
QUILTS!!!

The Complete Guide
To Quiltmaking

On the bed, see page 64. On the wall, see page 45. Wall quilt by Katie Prindle.

QUILTS! QUILTS!!
QUILTS!!!

*The Complete Guide
To Quiltmaking*

DIANA McCLUN AND LAURA NOWNES

 THE QUILT DIGEST PRESS
Simply the Best from NTC Publishing Group
Lincolnwood, Illinois U.S.A.

Editorial and production direction by Michael M. Kile.
Book and cover design by Kajun Graphics, San Francisco.
Photography by Sharon Risedorph, San Francisco.
Book editing and title conception by Harold Nadel.
Hand and computer graphics diagrams by Kandy Petersen.
Typographical composition in Bembo by Rock & Jones, Oakland, California.
Printed in Hong Kong.

Room stylings by Michael M. Kile, with Diana McClun, Marinda Brown
    Steward, Margaret Peters, Tricia Thomas and Bill Folk.
Appliqué instructions overseen by Adele Ingraham.
Quiltmaking techniques and ideas shared by Joyce Ganser, Mary Ellen Hopkins
    and Glendora Hutson.
Quilting and sewing assistance provided by Leona Hagen, Claire Jarratt,
    Sandy Klop, Ada Miller, Katie Prindle, Mary Helen Schwyn, Julie Shirley,
    Anna Venti and Kristina Volker.
Homes graciously lent by Nancy Callahan, Margaret Peters, Bernice Stone
    and Tricia Thomas.
Pattern name consultation by Cuesta Benberry and Barbara Brackman
Yardage calculation assistance by Diane Clements.
Advice on quiltmaking techniques by Dena Canty and Wanda Jones.

Invaluable manuscript review by Mary Ellen Hopkins, Roberta Horton, Mary
    Mashuta, Doreen Speckmann and Judy Warren.
Invaluable review of this book as a classroom text by Beryl Sue Coulson,
    Vickie McKenney, Darlene Roberts, June Simon and Sharon Yenter.

Diana and Laura thank their husbands, David and Bill, for their support and
    love.

Nineteenth Printing

Library of Congress Cataloging-in-Publication Data

McClun, Diana, 1934–
    Quilts! Quilts!! Quilts!!!
    ISBN 0-913327-16-6
    1. Quilting—Patterns.   2. Machine quilting—Patterns.
    I.   Nownes, Laura, 1953–   II. Title.
    TT833.M275   1988
    746.9'7   88-18563

Now published by NTC Publishing Group under ISBN 0-8442-2616-5

1995 Printing

Published by The Quilt Digest Press,
a division of NTC Publishing Group
4255 West Touhy Avenue
Lincolnwood (Chicago), Illinois 60646-1975, U.S.A.

5 6 7 8 9 0 WKT 19

On the wall, see page 55. On the rack, see pages 30, 55, 32 and 61. Wall quilt by Gai Perry.

See page 30.

On the bed, see page 68. On the wall, see pages 36 and 45. Wall quilt by Alex Anderson.

On the wall, see page 42. On the couch, see page 28.

See page 34.

On the couch, see page 44. Framed block on wall, see page 120.

See page 45.

See page 48.

On the wall, see page 157. On the crib, see pages 38 and 76.

All blocks in this planned Sampler are 12″.

TABLE OF CONTENTS

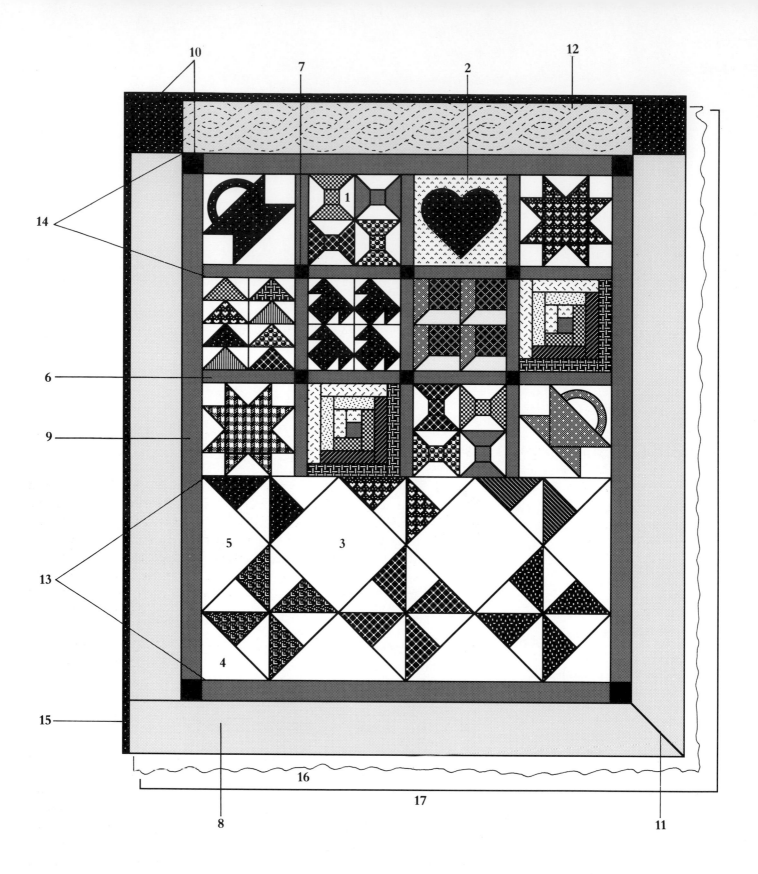

1. **Pieced block**
2. **Appliquéd block**
3. **Alternate block**
4. **Corner triangle**
5. **Side triangle**

6. **Sashing**
7. **Post**
8. **Outside border**
9. **Inside border**

10. **Corner block**
11. **Mitered corner**
12. **Quilting design**
13. **Diagonal setting**

14. **Straight setting**
15. **Binding**
16. **Batting**
17. **Backing**

## CHAPTER 1

THE ESSENTIALS

WHAT IS A QUILT?

A quilt is more than fabric, batting and stitches. It is a rare and wonderful creation of the soul which expresses our personal statements, our likes and dislikes, feelings, thoughts and loves. It is a bridge that encourages friendships. It supports our need for recognition, as we display it proudly to the applause of its admirers. And it links us with those who've stitched before and those who will follow as it gives a wordless but meaningful description of who we are and what we feel. A quilt is all these—and more: it is the embodiment of love.

Quilts give us a chance to express our need for giving. A dear member of the group was moving away, so Laura's quilting circle decided to express their love and treasured friendship. They constructed a quilt in her favorite colors, peach and green. Each quilter chose her favorite pattern, quilted her own stitches and signed her name, creating an enduring memento.

After years of teaching, we are always amazed that each student's quilt emerges as a thoroughly personal expression of herself as she selects colors, patterns and fabrics for a special purpose. One student was making her first quilt for the baby she was carrying. It was filled with favorite prints and colors. While the quilt was being constructed, the pregnancy was terminated, bringing grief and sorrow to this young woman. The quilt became a source of comfort: as she stitched each piece, she had quiet time to reflect about the child.

One of the dearest expressions of caring was the quilt top designed with 2″ squares representing the quiltmaker's entire fabric collection. A note was written on the border of the quilt: "Made by Mary Bragdon for Diana McClun. If you need any fabric, I have these."

There are many times when we need praise and recognition, and the quilt becomes the perfect bridge to people who will be impressed with the patterns, the colors, and the time we invested. Even if we don't exhibit in shows or contests, we like our family and friends to give us their approval. The husband of one beginning student kept displaying the unfinished quilt to guests: as the quilt progressed, the praise grew; now this quilt hangs proudly on the wall.

A quilt bridges generations of a family together. Diana grew up in Preston, Idaho, a small town near the Utah border. Her grandmothers, Louisa Nuffer and Ruby Hampton, were both quilters, and each of their quilts tells an autobiographical story. Grandmother Nuffer made her own wool batts and purchased scraps from the Utah Woolen Mills for her utilitarian quilts with dark flannel backs; Grandmother Hampton made beautiful, brightly patched quilts from cotton scraps. From the pieces her mother made for Diana's bridal quilt and for the quilts she sent to Kansas, Illinois and California to celebrate the arrival of each grandchild, it is obvious that she loved color, fabric and ornamentation and was a skilled seamstress.

This same sense of bonding occurred in Laura's family. At an early age she developed an unquenchable thirst for cloth to make doll clothes, from an old sheet or discarded shirt. She can remember spending hours in fabric shops with her mother, who didn't sew, but who encouraged her. This mother-daughter team adored being with each other. During her adolescence, every school sewing class was a step towards understanding the exciting processes of cutting, pinning, picking colors and stitching. By the time she met Diana, Laura had graduated from college and had years of sewing experience. It was in a color class Diana was teaching at her shop, Empty Spools, that they found and shared a common bond. Soon Laura was quilting and teaching classes at Empty Spools, giving every minute to the well-being of the business, helping quilters with problems, choosing colors, organizing fashion and gallery shows to honor quiltmakers. Laura's quilting friends secretly made a beautiful appliqué and trapunto bridal quilt for her marriage to Bill. However, it was Laura who designed and stitched yards and yards of French lace and swiss batiste into a magnificent wedding dress. And now there are quilts for her daughter Sara, quilts for the family and quilts for friends. Those childhood experiences, the stories told to her of her grandmother's sewing expertise, her mother's love and encouragement, all create this heritage of women that is so much a part of her life.

We both share with you the same joy and love of creativity our ancestors had. Now it's time to do what we do best—detail the construction of a quilt from start to finish, so you too can have the experiences only a quilt can bring.

Diana & Laura

HOW TO USE THIS BOOK

Let's take the mystery out of quiltmaking. If you are a beginner, you need to be willing to learn the few—but essential—basics. If you have already made a quilt, you know it requires some diligence and patience (attributes many people think unattainable, yet develop as they become quiltmakers!). But there is no mystery. People who had considered themselves lacking in creativity have produced quilts of great beauty. You can, too!

Everything you need to know is here. This book deliberately includes patterns that beginning quiltmakers can complete successfully, as well as designs an experienced quiltmaker will enjoy working with. There are popular and traditional patterns—and all the instructions for the techniques required to make them.

The patterns are arranged in a progressive sequence, incorporating new designs and utilizing more difficult techniques as you move from the simpler patterns to the more complex. Some patterns will require more precise work than others, but with careful work all can be completed by the quiltmaker who begins with the simpler patterns, moving onward as experience warrants. There are years of joyous quiltmaking within these pages.

You can select one of the patterns and make a quilt or you can make a variety of pattern blocks and incorporate them into a *Sampler* quilt similar to the examples shown on page 9. (Choose one you like or make up your own combination of blocks.) Using some of the quick techniques included here, you can complete a quilt in a reasonable period of time and move on to another one that interests you.

Here is a recommended series of steps to help you best use this book:

Step 1. Read first, then quilt. Read through the entire book from start to finish to get an overall idea of the quiltmaking process. Don't jump around. All the important information is not given in the first few pages but developed progressively throughout. Next, re-read the book, spending time on the practice exercises. These are intended as learning experiences to familiarize you with basic quiltmaking techniques before you begin on your first quilt. (If you are an experienced quiltmaker, you can skip some of these exercises, but we urge you to do the ones involving new time-saving techniques we have developed.) Instructions for making the quilts assume that you have knowledge of the techniques, including those developed in the practice exercises. If you do, you will be happy with your results.

Since this is intended as a workbook, wide margins and spaces for your personal notes have been given. The Table of Contents serves also as an index to the book, with specific page listings. It is conveniently placed at the front for ready reference. We have highlighted *helpful hints* (✶) and *warnings* (◩) we feel are important. You should feel free to highlight other points yourself and add personal observations. Then, you can decide which techniques you feel most comfortable with—quick methods, traditional methods, or a combination of the two.

Step 2. Choose a pattern. Look through Chapter 2, "Choosing a Pattern." For a positive quilting experience, we recommend that a beginner make one of the quilts requiring only strips (such as *Fence Rail* or *Roman Square*) as a first quilt. Work and become comfortable with its techniques before moving on to patterns with squares, triangles or diamonds. If you are an experienced quiltmaker, choose freely from among the many patterns offered. Remember: the patterns in Chapter 2 are arranged in a progressive sequence.

Step 3. Determine the size of your quilt. Decide on the finished size of the quilt you wish to make. How do you intend to use it? Will it be used on a bed or as a wall hanging? Once you've determined this, turn to the pattern you selected in Chapter 2. There you will find a chart that succinctly gives you the total number of pattern blocks and suggested border widths recommended for the setting and size quilt you wish to make. You will also find convenient yardage specifications for all quilt sizes and settings.

Step 4. Decide on a color scheme. For most quiltmakers, this is the most difficult decision. Since we can't see the finished quilt but can only speculate upon what it will look like, this is an especially difficult task for the beginner. Fabric suggestions have been included with each pattern in Chapter 2, and guidelines, exercises and examples are included in Chapter 3, which deals extensively with the color selection process. Take the time to study Chapter 3 and you will create a quilt that is pleasing to you. Chapter 3 is one we recommend to all quiltmakers.

Step 5. Prepare your fabric. The procedures necessary for preparing your fabric for cutting and sewing are discussed in Chapter 4. Whether you are experienced or a novice, take the time to treat your fabric with the required care before you begin to cut.

Step 6. Make your quilt. Chapters 5 through 10 include step-by-step instructions with diagrams and illustrations of the various techniques required for making the quilts in this book. Study the instructions, work on the practice exercises if you have not yet done so and become familiar with the necessary techniques before beginning your quilt.

Whenever possible, we have used a 12″ quilt block for the patterns we selected for this book. We've included popular and classic traditional patterns. *And everything you need to know to make every quilt in this book is included here.* Each pattern in this book includes the following:

1. *Complete instructions* for making the quilt.

2. At least one color photograph of the pattern as an entire quilt.

3. A diagram of the individual pattern block.

4. A sew order block which indicates the order in which the individual pieces are sewn together.

5. Yardage requirements for a variety of bed and wall sizes.

6. Suggested fabrics.

7. Template patterns for each individual part of the pattern block. These template patterns can be used for both machine and hand work.

So, remember: there is no mystery. Relax. The more you sew, the more you will know. And the more you will enjoy. *Quilts! Quilts!! Quilts!!!* was created for your enjoyment. And there is no more enjoyable pastime than quiltmaking. It is an elixir for the soul. Happy Quilting!

QUILTMAKING INSTRUCTORS. We have included a class outline on page 157. We have found it successful for making the scrap *Sampler* quilt (see page 9, on nursery wall) in our basic quiltmaking classes. It contains patterns from this book. Utilizing your experience, the outline and this book as your classroom text, your classes will be smash successes.

UNDERSTANDING FABRIC

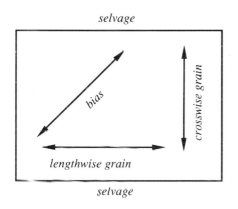

PARTS OF FABRIC

Selvage. The lengthwise finished edges of a woven fabric.

Grain. The lengthwise and crosswise threads of a woven fabric used in its construction. The lengthwise grain runs parallel to the selvage edges of the fabric. This has the least amount of stretch. The crosswise grain runs perpendicular to the selvage edges and has a little more stretch than the lengthwise grain.

Bias. The diagonal of a woven fabric in which a true 45-degree angle is formed. The bias has the greatest amount of stretch.

Fiber content is important when you purchase fabric for your quilts. The content determines the way in which the fabric will respond to manipulation. We strongly recommend that you purchase 100% cotton fabrics. Cotton is strong when wet, irons easily at high temperatures, creases easily, absorbs moisture and wears well. Read the label on the bolt-end of the fabric to determine the fiber content. Quilters need to purchase good-quality, colorfast cotton fabric that is treated with finishes to control shrinkage, resist soil and resist wrinkling.

Not only is the type and quality of the fabric important, but also the printed or woven surface design—and, of course, the color. You must like the fabric; in fact, you should love it and want to live with it. The design should be pleasing to you. Check to see if there is a one-way direction to the design; this will affect the way the fabric will be cut, and you may need to purchase extra yardage to allow for cutting fabrics such as plaids and stripes (whether horizontal, vertical or diagonal). Take a few minutes to analyze the fabric before purchasing it.

The scale of the design and the spaces between the designs (called the background) are also important considerations. Is the design large, medium or small? Is the background area prominent? How will the design look when cut into small pieces? If the design is too widely spaced, you may lose it. Look at the following samples and keep them in mind when you are shopping.

GEOMETRIC: Circles, ovals, spirals, squares, rectangles, triangles, diamonds, stripes, zigzags, herringbone, plaids, checks, etc. These will work well, but extra yardage and cutting time are required.

STYLIZED: A stylized design is one in which the shapes are distorted from the real object. The original source is generally recognizable but the shape is exaggerated or simplified; it looks unnatural.

REALISTIC: A realistic or naturalistic design depicts real objects or shapes in a natural manner. Human, animal and plant forms will look real. These have been favorite designs for quiltmaking. There is a wide selection of floral designs. They are generally easy to use.

ABSTRACT: Abstract patterns have little or no reference to real objects. Distinctions between abstract and geometric are sometimes blurred and it becomes difficult to categorize them. These cut up into interesting pieces.

COMBINATIONS: Some fabrics can be a combination of one or more of the four categories.

STITCHES AND KNOTS

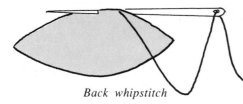

Backstitch

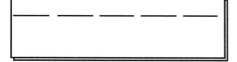

Back whipstitch

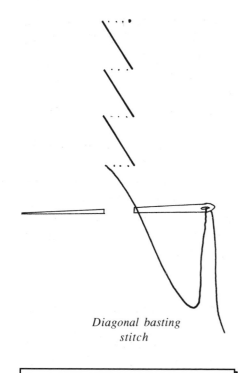

Running basting stitch

Backstitch. These are very short stitches used at the beginning or end of a line of stitching to secure threads. These are used instead of knots. Leave a 1″ tail of thread at each end of the stitching line. Use a single strand of thread.

Back whipstitch. For hand appliqué work, use a single strand of thread and secure one end with a knot. With the right side of the design facing up, bring the needle and thread up from the underside out through the folded edge in the design. Insert the tip of the needle directly behind and a little below the point where the thread emerges. Without pulling the thread through, slant the needle and bring it to the top side through the folded edge in the design, approximately 1/16″ away from the previous stitch. Pull the thread through.

Basting stitches. Temporary stitches used to hold fabric in place. Use a single strand of thread.

    Running basting stitch. Use the same technique as described in running stitch, but with a longer stitch.

    Diagonal basting stitch. Long, parallel diagonal stitches on the right side of the quilt, joined on the wrong side by horizontal stitches.

Running stitch. A short, even stitch used for hand piecing.

Slip stitch. This is a small, almost invisible, stitch used to secure a folded edge to a flat surface. Use a single strand of thread and secure one end with a knot. To secure a binding, bring the needle and thread up through the fold in the binding. Insert the needle directly behind where the thread emerged, catching only a few threads of the backing fabric. Without pulling the thread through, bring the needle up through the fold in the binding approximately 1/8″ away from the previous stitch.

Square knot. Bring the left thread over and around the right thread. Then, cross the right thread in front of the left and bring it through the loop. Pull both ends to tighten the knot.

Diagonal basting stitch

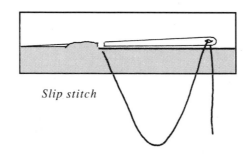

Slip stitch

Square knot

Running stitch

VOCABULARY

Alternate block set. Pieced blocks which are combined or alternated with plain blocks.

Appliqué. A design made by cutting shapes of one or more fabrics and *applying* them to the surface of another.

Backing. The fabric which forms the bottom layer of the quilt.

Backstitch. See definition and instructions on page 20.

Back whipstitch. See definition and instructions on page 20.

Baste. A means of loosely securing layers together temporarily. Definitions for **running basting** and **diagonal basting stitches** are given on page 20.

Batting. A term used for the filling that goes between the quilt top and the backing. It provides thickness and warmth to the quilt.

Bias. The diagonal of a woven fabric in which a true 45-degree angle is formed. The bias has the greatest amount of stretch.

Binding. A narrow strip of fabric used to enclose the raw edges of the quilt top, batting and backing. It can be cut on either the straight grain or the bias.

Block. See **Pattern.** Most of the patterns in this book are made up into 12″ blocks.

Border. Plain, pieced or appliquéd band(s) of fabric surrounding the central section of the quilt top.

Chain/chaining. A term used to describe the method of connecting sewn pairs of pattern pieces, one behind the other, in the sewing machine, without breaking the thread connecting them.

Concave. Curved like the inner surface of a sphere.

Convex. Curved like the exterior of a sphere.

Directional fabric. Fabric having a directional print (either horizontal, vertical or diagonal).

Drafted pattern. Outline of the individual parts of a pattern block, made on graph paper.

Grain. The lengthwise and crosswise threads of a woven fabric. The lengthwise threads (or **lengthwise grain**) run parallel to the selvage edges of the fabric. This has the least amount of stretch. The crosswise threads (or **crosswise grain**) run perpendicular to the selvage edges and have a little more stretch than the lengthwise grain.

Grainline. The lengthwise grain of the fabric.

Grid. Squares of uniform size.

Ground fabric. A fabric or fabrics used as the background in a pattern block.

Hand quilting. Small running stitches which hold the three layers of the quilt together, either following a design which has been marked on the quilt top or following the outline of a pieced or appliquéd block.

Layering. The process of placing the three layers of the quilt together.

Loft. The springiness, or fluffiness, of a fiber.

Machine quilting. Machine stitches which hold the three layers of the quilt together.

(Continued on page 24)

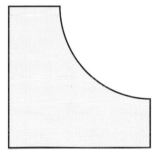

Concave

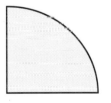

Convex

EQUIPMENT AND SUPPLIES

1. Pressing surface
2. Steam iron
3. Light-colored towel
4. Masking tape
5. Drafting tape
6. Template plastic
7. Ultra-fine sandpaper
8. Drafting compass
9. Graph paper, 1/8″ grid
10. Plain paper
11. C-Thru plastic 1″ × 6″ ruler (B-50)
12. C-Thru plastic 2″ × 18″ ruler (B-85)
13. Cutting board
14. Rotary cutter
15. Even-feed walking foot for sewing machine
16. Sewing machine
17. Sewing-machine needle, #12 (#80)
18. Fabric scissors, 8″
19. Paper scissors
20. Small scissors
21. Small box for fabric pieces
22. Ribbon
23. Reducing glass
24. Plastic circle template
25. Wide plastic ruler (with marked 45-degree angle) to be used as a cutting edge
26. Quilting thread
27. Ultra-fine permanent pens, black and red
28. Artist's soft pencils, white, gray and silver
29. Lead pencils, #2.5 and #3
30. Pencil sharpener
31. Eraser
32. Tweezers
33. Seam ripper
34. Beeswax
35. Needle threader
36. Needle grabber
37. Cotton thread
38. Thimble
39. Needles, #9, #10 and #12 Betweens
40. Hand-sewing needle
41. Cotton darning needle, #1
42. Plastic or metal tape measure
43. Cotton/polyester or nylon filament thread
44. Perle cotton thread
45. Sequin pins, 3/4″ steel
46. Glass-head pins
47. Pin cushion
48. Steel safety pins, #1
49. Quilting hoop or frame
50. Quilting design template
51. Batting
52. Polyester felted fleece or white flannel, two yards, for design board
53. Bias bar or flat metal strip, 1/4″ wide
54. Plexiglas rod, 1/4″ square
55. Plastic right-angle triangle

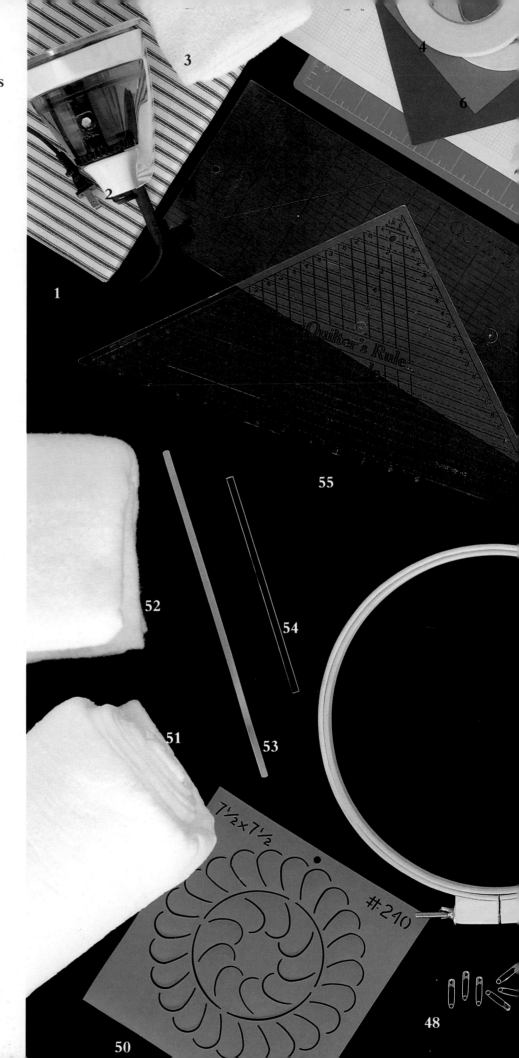

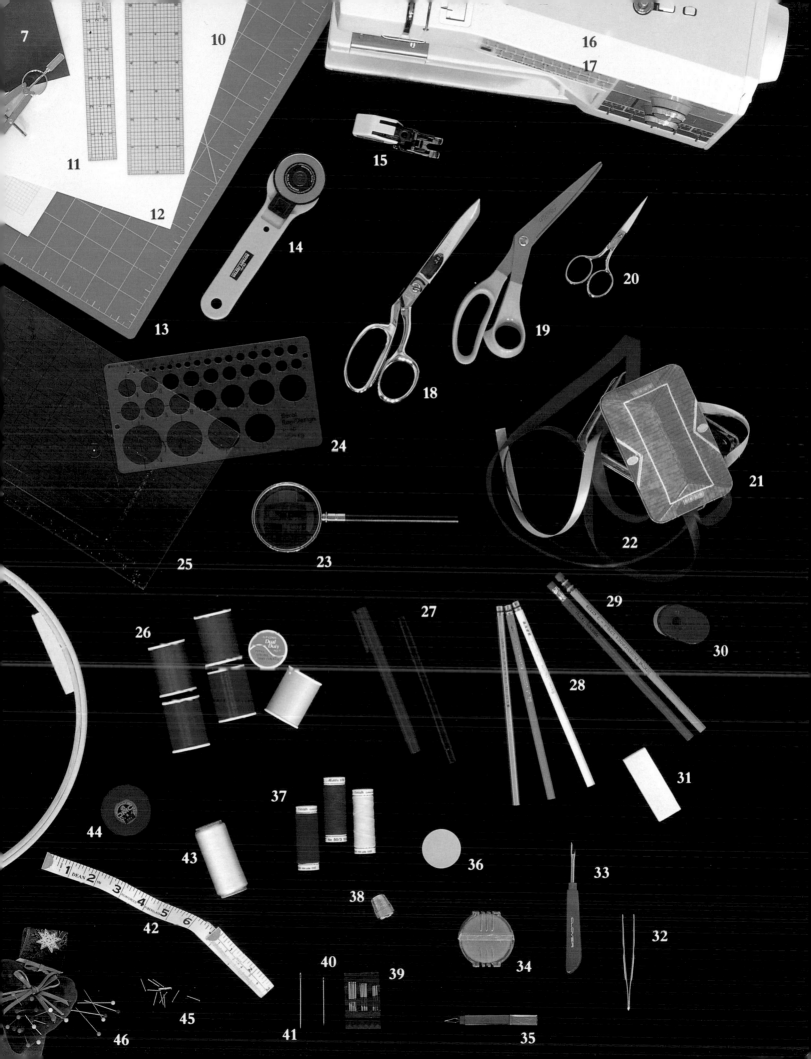

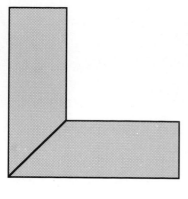

Miter

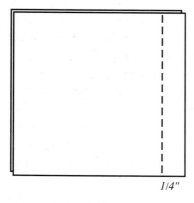

1/4"

Seam allowance

Miter. Vertical and horizontal strips of fabric are joined at 45-degree angles, forming a 90-degree corner. Mitered corners can be used in constructing borders.

Non-directional fabric. A printed fabric without a direction, such as an all-over print.

Pattern. Any design of a quilt usually repeated several times on the quilt top. Sometimes referred to as "design."

Perle cotton. A two-ply cotton yarn with a high twist and a silk-like finish.

Piecing/pieced block. Pieces of cut cloth sewn together to produce a pattern, usually in the form of a block.

Posts. Squares of fabric joining sashing to sashing. See page 12.

Quilt top. The top layer of the quilt. It can be pieced, appliquéd or a combination of the two.

Quilting/quilting stitches. Stitches used to secure the three layers of the quilt together. The quilting can be done by either hand or machine.

Running stitch. See definition and instructions on page 20.

Sashing. The strip of fabric used between blocks to separate and set them together. See page 12.

Seam. The stitched junction of two pieces of fabric, right sides together, with a 1/4″ seam allowance. Can be done by either hand or machine.

Seam allowance. The distance between the cut edge of the fabrics and the stitching line. In quiltmaking this is 1/4″.

Selvage. The finished edges of a woven fabric on the lengthwise threads.

Set/setting. The arrangement in which individual blocks are sewn together. A **diagonal** or **straight** setting is commonly used. See page 12.

Sew order. The sequence of sewing individual pieces together to form a unit.

Slip stitch. Definition and instructions are given on page 20.

Square knot. Definition and instructions are given on page 20.

Template. An individual model of a part of a pattern block made from template plastic.

Tying. A quick method of securing the three layers of the quilt together.

CHAPTER 2

CHOOSING A PATTERN

The patterns in this chapter are organized in a progressive fashion; the easiest patterns come first. Beginning quiltmakers are urged to start with one of the patterns which require only strip piecing: *Roman Square, Fence Rail* or *Log Cabin*.

Yardage charts and fabric. We have listed generous amounts of fabric in the yardage charts. Our experience tells us that there are few things in quiltmaking as frustrating as nearing the end of a quilt project only to discover that you are 1/4 yard short of an essential fabric. Use the extra fabric that will be left over to begin—or replenish—your scrap bag for future quilt projects. For border fabrics, we have given enough fabric so that you can miter your corners, if desired.

Cutting charts. It is important that you cut your fabric *in the order listed in these charts, so that you do not cut into a length you will need elsewhere.*

Hand or machine work. We have listed template numbers *and* quick-cutting methods with each pattern. Thus, these pattern instructions can be used for either hand or machine work.

Borders. We have given suggested border widths in the cutting charts. These are only suggestions. If you feel confident enough, please determine your own borders and their widths. This may, however, change the amount of backing fabric required.

Quilt sizes (for example, 61″ × 90″) are given as width × length.

Dimensions. All dimensions have been rounded *up* to the nearest whole number.

ROMAN SQUARE

Diana McClun and Laura Nownes

Block size: 4½″
Techniques: Strip piecing or Template 2b
Setting: Diagonal
Fabric suggestions: Variety of scraps, twice as many darks as lights. Fabric for border to complement your finished blocks.

	Crib/Wall	Twin	Double	Queen	King
Finished size	40″×53″	67″×86″	82″×89″	88″×94″	106″×93″
Blocks set	5×7	8×11	11×12	12×13	15×13
# pieced blocks	59	158	242	288	363
# side triangles	20	34	42	46	52

YARDAGE

	Crib/Wall	Twin	Double	Queen	King
Block fabrics: scraps to total	2	4	5½	6½	8¼
Side and corner triangles	1¼	1½	1½	1½	1¾
Border	2	2½	3	3¼	3½
Backing and binding	3½	5⅜	8¼	8½	8½

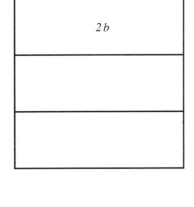

CUTTING

	Crib/Wall	Twin	Double	Queen	King
Template 2b	177	474	726	864	1089
– OR –					
Quick: number of strips	23	60	92	108	137
For side triangles: number of pieces	5	9	11	12	13
For corner triangles: number of pieces	2	2	2	2	2
Border: width	4½"	4½"	4½"	4½"	4½"
Backing: number of lengths	2	2	3	3	3

Quick-cutting: Cut all of your quilt-top fabrics (except borders) crossgrain.
- For 2b: Cut 2" wide strips.
- For side triangles: Cut 8½" squares. Then cut each square into quarters diagonally.
- For corner triangles: Cut 6" squares. Then cut each square in half diagonally.

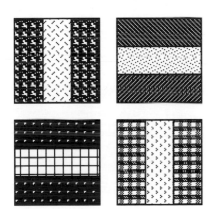

CONSTRUCTION

1. Sew a variety of different combinations of units. Each unit consists of one light between two dark strips.
2. Cut each unit apart every 5".
3. Sew order: see diagram.

Sampler Roman Square

NOTE: For the arrangement shown in the planned *Sampler* quilt on page 9 use Template 1b or, for quick methods, cut strips 1½" wide. Construct as directed above and sew together exactly as shown in the diagram.

FENCE RAIL

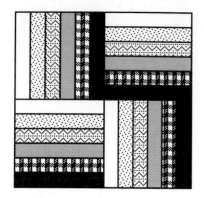

Block size: 12″
Techniques: Strip piecing or Template 1e
Setting: Straight
Fabric suggestions: Six fabrics for blocks, graduated from light to dark. Border fabrics that complement your finished blocks.

	Crib/Wall	Twin	Double	Queen	King
Finished size	44″×56″	66″×90″	80″×92″	84″×96″	106″×94″
Blocks set	3×4	4×6	5×6	5×6	7×6
Total blocks	12	24	30	30	42

YARDAGE

	Crib/Wall	Twin	Double	Queen	King
Block fabrics: *each* of six	½	1	1⅛	1⅛	1½
Inside border	1¾	2⅜	2⅜	2⅜	2¾
Outside border	2	2¾	3	3⅛	3½
Backing and binding	3½	5⅜	5½	6	9¼

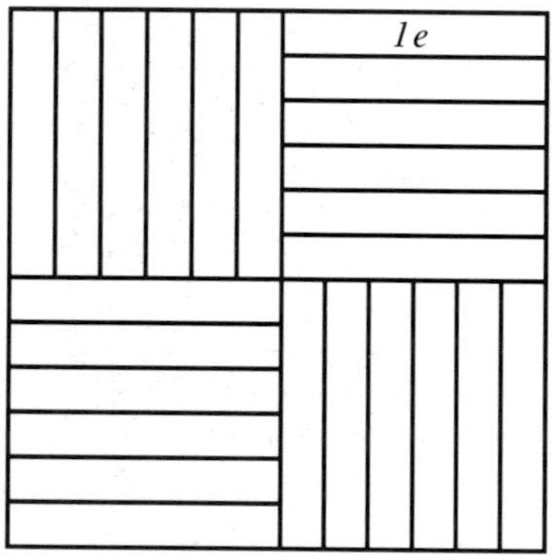

CUTTING

	Crib/Wall	Twin	Double	Queen	King
Template 1e, *each* of every block fabric	48	96	120	120	168
Inside border: width	2″	2″	2″	2½″	2½″
Outside border: width	3½″	8″	9″	10½″	9½″
Backing: number of lengths	2	2	2	2	3

Quick-cutting: Cut all of your quilt-top fabrics (except borders) crossgrain, in 1½″-wide strips.

CONSTRUCTION

1. Sew six strips together, from light to dark, to make each set. Cut the sets apart every 6½″.
2. Sew order: see diagram.

✱ *Helpful hint:* See *Fence Rail* practice exercise in Chapter 5 for help.

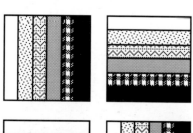

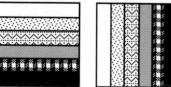

Diana McClun and Laura Nownes

LOG CABIN:
LIGHT AND DARK VARIATION

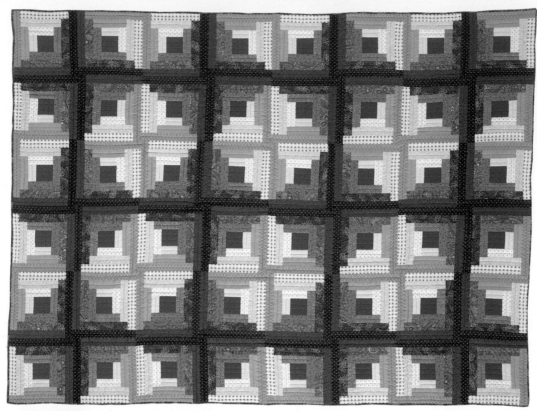

Diana McClun and Laura Nownes

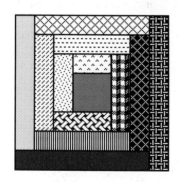

Block size: 12″
Techniques: Quick-cutting or Templates 1n, 1o, 2a, 2b, 2c, 2d, 2e, 4c
Setting: Straight, to form light and dark variation of pattern
Fabric suggestions: One fabric for all center squares (chimneys), six light fabrics and six dark fabrics.

	Crib/Wall	Twin	Double	Queen	King
Finished size	36″×48″	60″×84″	84″×84″	84″×96″	108″×96″
Blocks set	3×4	5×7	7×7	7×8	9×8
Total blocks	12	35	49	56	72

YARDAGE

	Crib/Wall	Twin	Double	Queen	King
Center and first light, *each*	¼	⅜	½	½	⅝
Second light and first dark, *each*	¼	⅜	½	½	⅝
Second dark and third light, *each*	¼	½	⅝	¾	⅞
Fourth light and third dark, *each*	¼	⅝	¾	⅞	1⅛

	Crib/Wall	Twin	Double	Queen	King
Fourth dark and fifth light, *each*	⅜	⅝	⅞	1⅛	1¼
Sixth light, fifth dark and sixth dark, *each*	⅜	⅞	1⅛	1¼	1½
Backing	1½	5	7½	8½	9½
Binding	⅜	½	⅝	⅝	¾

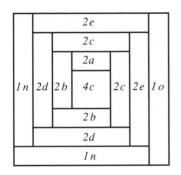

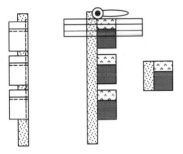

Step 1

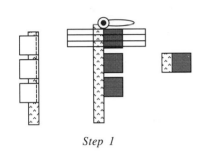

Step 2

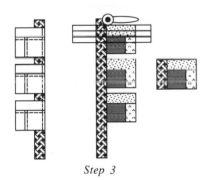

Step 3

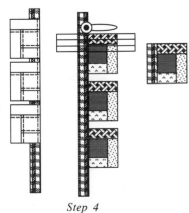

Step 4

CUTTING

	Crib/Wall	Twin	Double	Queen	King
For all templates: number of pieces, *each*	12	35	49	56	72

– OR –

Quick-cutting: Cut all of your quilt-top fabrics crossgrain.
 • For 4c: Cut 3½″-wide strips. Then cut to 3½″ squares.
 • For all other pieces: Cut 2″-wide strips. Then cut to the length of the templates.

CONSTRUCTION

1. With right sides together, sew the center squares (4c) to a strip of the first light (2a) fabric. Press towards the first light fabric. Cut the resulting units apart as shown in the diagram.

2. With right sides together, sew the units formed in Step 1 to a strip of the second light (2b) fabric. Press towards the second light fabric. Cut as shown in the diagram.

3. With right sides together, sew the units formed in Step 2 to a strip of the first dark (2b) fabric. Press towards the first dark fabric. Cut as shown in the diagram.

4. In a manner similar to Steps 2 and 3, sew the remaining strips to the units as follows: second dark (2c), third light (2c), fourth light (2d), third dark (2d), fourth dark (2e), fifth light (2e), sixth light (1n), fifth dark (1n), sixth dark (1o).

All individual blocks are constructed in the same manner. You can vary the arrangement in order to create different designs. Two possibilities are:

Straight Furrow   Barn Raising

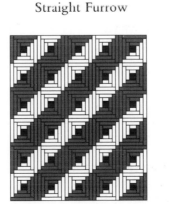

NOTE: For the arrangement shown in the planned *Sampler* on page 9 use Templates 1a, 1b, 1c, 1d, 1e and 3c or, for quick methods, cut center 2½″ square and all strips 1½″ wide.

DOUBLE NINE PATCH

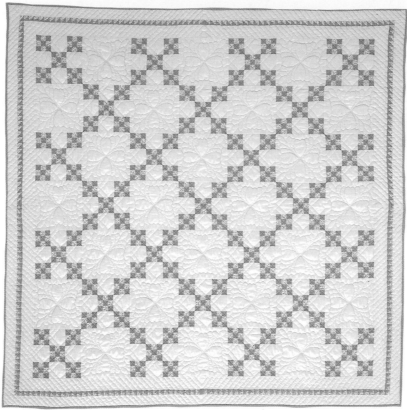

Rosalee Sanders

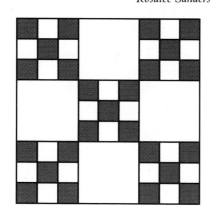

Block size: 9″

Techniques: Strip piecing, quick-cutting and half-square triangles or Templates 3a, 4c, 2k

Setting: Straight, with alternate blocks

Fabric suggestions: One light, one medium and one dark

	Crib/Wall	Twin	Double	Queen	King
Finished size	45″ × 45″	77″ × 77″	89″ × 89″	95″ × 95″	113″ × 113″
Blocks set	5 × 5	7 × 7	9 × 9	9 × 9	11 × 11
# pieced blocks	13	25	41	41	61
# alternate blocks	12	24	40	40	60

YARDAGE

	Crib/Wall	Twin	Double	Queen	King
Light fabric, including border	1⅞	5¼	7	7¼	9¾
For pieced blocks and sawtooth border:					
Color one (medium)	¾	2	2¾	2¾	3½
Color two (dark)	¾	2¼	3¼	3¼	4
Backing and binding	3	4¾	8	8½	10

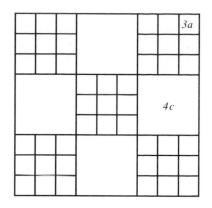

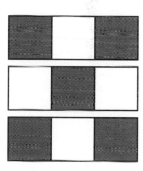

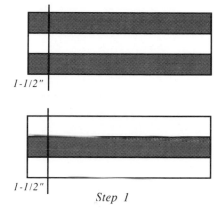

1-1/2"

1-1/2"

Step 1

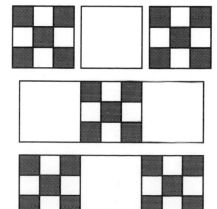

Step 2

Step 3

NOTE: There are no borders allowed on the crib size and no outside borders allowed on the double size.

CUTTING

	Crib/Wall	Twin	Double	Queen	King
Light fabric:					
Inside border: four *each*					
Width	—	3½"	3½"	3½"	3½"
Length	—	78"	96"	96"	114"
Outside border: four *each*					
Width	—	3½"	—	3½"	3½"
Length	—	86"	—	104"	122"
Alternate blocks: number of pieces	12	24	40	40	60
Template 4c	52	100	164	164	244
— OR —					
Quick: number of strips	5	9	14	14	21
Medium fabric: **Template 3a**	260	500	820	820	1220
— OR —					
Quick: number of strips	10	18	30	30	44
Dark fabric: **Template 3a**	325	625	1025	1025	1525
— OR —					
Quick: number of strips	12	23	37	37	55
Template 2k for sawtooth border: medium and dark, *each*	—	288	360	360	432
— OR —					
Quick: number of pieces *each*, medium and dark	—	5	6	6	8
Backing: number of lengths	2	2	3	3	3

Quick-cutting: Cut all of your quilt-top fabrics (except borders) crossgrain.
- For alternate blocks: Cut 9½" squares.
- For 3a: Cut 1½"-wide strips.
- For 4c: Cut 3½"-wide strips. Then cut to 3½" squares.
- For 2k: Cut 10" × 12" pieces.

CONSTRUCTION

1. Sew two combinations of 3a strips. Cut apart every 1½".
2. To construct *Nine Patch* units: see diagram.
3. Sew order: see diagram.
4. Sawtooth border: Sew the medium and dark 2k pieces together to make half-square triangle units or, for quick method, the grid size is 1⅞".

DOUBLE NINE PATCH

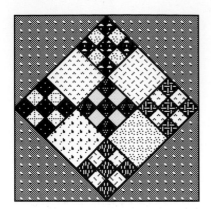

Block size: 12¾"
Techniques: Quick-cutting and strip piecing or Templates 3a, 4c
Setting: Straight
Fabric suggestions: Scraps for pieced *Nine Patch* and plain square units. Two fabrics for large triangles.

	Crib/Wall	Twin	Double	Queen	King
Finished size	50"×50"	70"×83"	79"×92"	83"×96"	101"×101"
Blocks set	3×3	4×5	5×6	5×6	6×6
Total blocks	9	20	30	30	36

YARDAGE

	Crib/Wall	Twin	Double	Queen	King
For *Nine Patch* units: scraps to total	1	1⅝	2½	2½	2¾
Plain square units: scraps to total	⅝	1	1¼	1¼	1½
Large triangles: *each* **of two fabrics**	½	1	1⅜	1⅜	1¾
Inside border	1¼	2	2⅜	2⅜	2⅜
Outside border	1¾	2¾	3	3	3¼
Backing and binding	3	4¾	5¼	8	8¾

CUTTING

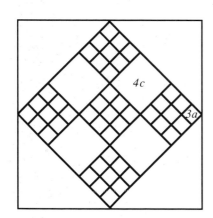

	Crib/Wall	Twin	Double	Queen	King
For *Nine Patch* units: **Template 3a**	405	900	1350	1350	1620
– OR – **Quick:** number of strips	16	33	49	49	59
For plain square units: Template 4c	36	80	120	120	144
– OR – **Quick:** number of strips	3	7	10	10	12
Large triangles: number of pieces, *each* **of two fabrics**	9	20	30	30	36
Inside border: width	1½"	2"	2"	2"	2½"
Outside border: width	5"	8½"	6½"	8½"	10½"
Backing: number of lengths	2	2	2	3	3

Quick-cutting: Cut all of your quilt-top fabrics (except borders) crossgrain.

- For 3a: Cut 1½″-wide strips.
- For 4c: Cut 3½″-wide strips. Then cut to 3½″ squares.
- For large triangles: Cut 7½″ squares. Then cut each square in half diagonally.

CONSTRUCTION

1. Sew several different combinations of 3a strips. Cut every 1½″.
2. To construct *Nine Patch* units: see diagram.
3. Sew order: see diagram.
4. The large triangles will be a little too big. Trim the completed block to 13¼″.

NOTE: For the 6″ *Nine Patch* blocks shown in the scrap *Sampler* on page 9, use Template 3c or, for quick method, cut three 2½″ × 15″ strips each, light and dark. Sew two combinations, cutting apart every 2½″, and construct as shown in Step 2 above.

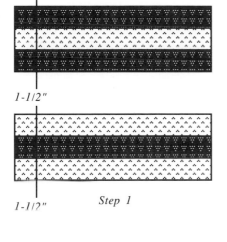

1-1/2″

1-1/2″   *Step 1*

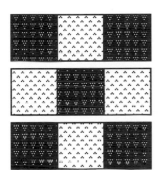

Step 2

Step 3

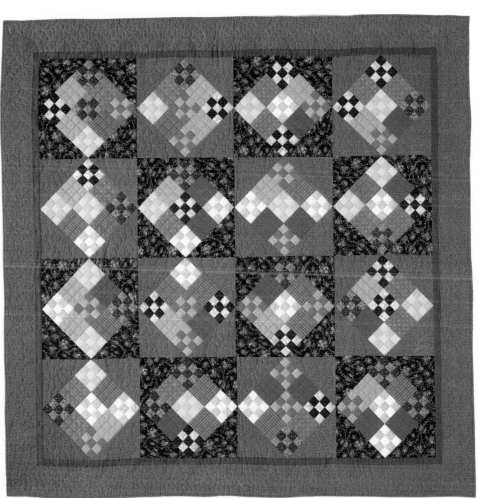

Diana McClun and Laura Nownes

PINWHEEL

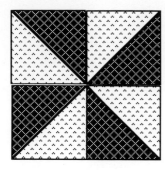

Block size: 5″

Techniques: Quick-cutting and double half-square triangles or Templates 2o and 3g

Setting: Diagonal

Fabric suggestions: Light and dark for pieced block. Medium for alternate block. Fabrics for borders to complement your finished blocks.

	Crib/Wall	Twin	Double	Queen	King
Finished size	49″×63″	77″×92″	85″×99″	92″×99″	106″×99″
Blocks set	5×7	9×11	10×12	11×12	13×12
# pieced blocks	35	99	120	132	156
# alternate blocks	24	80	99	110	132
# side triangles	20	36	40	42	46

YARDAGE

	Crib/Wall	Twin	Double	Queen	King
Pinwheel **blocks:** each **of two fabrics**	1¼	2¼	2¼	2¾	3¼
Alternate blocks and side triangles	1⅝	3¼	3½	3½	5¾
Borders: *each* **of three fabrics**	2⅛	2⅞	3⅛	3⅛	3⅜
Backing and binding	3¾	5⅜	8⅝	8⅝	9¼

CUTTING

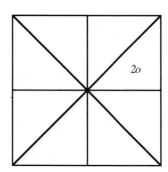

2o

	Crib/Wall	Twin	Double	Queen	King
Template 2o: light and dark, *each*	140	396	480	528	624
– OR –					
Quick: number of pieces	3	7	8	9	11
Alternate block: Template 3g	24	80	99	110	132
– OR –					
Quick: number of strips	4	12	15	16	19
Side triangles: number of pieces	5	9	10	11	12
Corner triangles: number of pieces	2	2	2	2	2
Inside border: width	1¼″	1¼″	1¼″	1¼″	1¼″
Middle border: width	1¾″	1¾″	1¾″	1¾″	1¾″
Outside border: width	5″	5″	5″	5″	5″
Backing: number of lengths	2	2	3	3	3

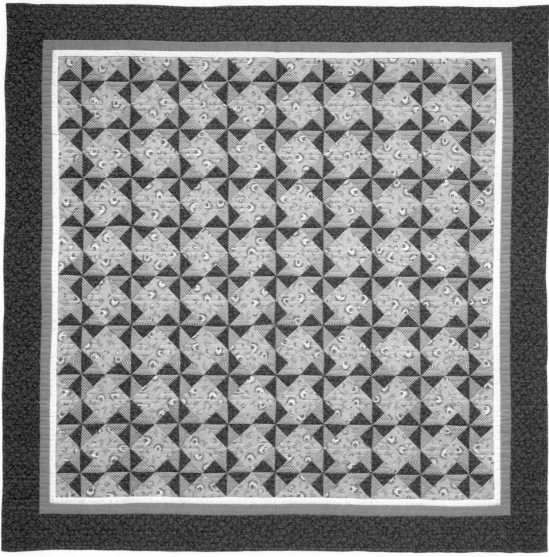

Pat Callis

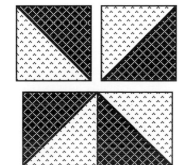

Quick-cutting: Cut all of your quilt-top fabrics (except borders) crossgrain.
  • For 2o: Cut 18″ × 22″ pieces.
  • For 3g: Cut 5½″-wide strips. Then cut to 5½″ squares.
  • For side triangles: Cut 9″ squares. Then cut each square into quarters diagonally.
  • For corner triangles: Cut 6½″ squares. Then cut each square in half diagonally.

CONSTRUCTION

1. Sew half-square triangle units from the light and dark 2o pieces. For quick method, the grid size is 3⅜″.

2. Sew order: see diagram.

✲ *Helpful hint:* See the *Pinwheel* practice exercise in Chapter 5 for help with construction.

Note: Use Template 2n for making the *Pinwheel* blocks in the quilt shown on the wall above the bed on page 6 or, for quick method, the grid size is 2⅞″.

T BLOCKS

Diana McClun and Laura Nownes

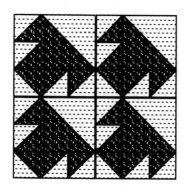

Block size: 12″

Techniques: Strip piecing and double half-square triangles or Templates 2n and 2q

Setting: Straight

Fabric suggestions: Variety of light fabrics for light *T Blocks*. Variety of medium and dark fabrics for darker *T Blocks*. Fabric for inside border that complements your finished blocks.

	Crib/Wall	Twin	Double	Queen	King
Finished size	44″×56″	56″×56″	72″×84″	84″×96″	108″×84″
Blocks set	3×4	4×4	5×6	6×7	8×7
Total blocks	12	16	30	42	56

YARDAGE

	Crib/Wall	Twin	Double	Queen	King
Light: for *T Blocks* and sawtooth border, scraps to total	1⅞	2¼	3⅝	4⅞	6¼
Dark: for *T Blocks* and sawtooth border, scraps to total	1⅞	2¼	3⅝	4⅞	6¼
Inside border	1½	2¼	2¼	2⅜	2⅝
Backing and binding	3⅜	3⅜	5	9	9½

CUTTING

	Crib/Wall	Twin	Double	Queen	King
Template 2q: light and dark, *each*	48	64	120	168	224
—OR—					
Quick: light and dark, number of strips, *each*	3	4	8	11	14
Template 2n: light and dark, *each*	336	428	752	1016	1320
—OR—					
Quick: light and dark, number of pieces, *each*	7	9	16	22	28
Inside border: width	2½"	2½"	4½"	4½"	4½"
Inside corner blocks: four squares *each*	2½"	2½"	4½"	4½"	4½"
Outside corner blocks: four squares *each*	2½"	2½"	2½"	2½"	2½"
Backing: number of lengths	2	2	2	3	3

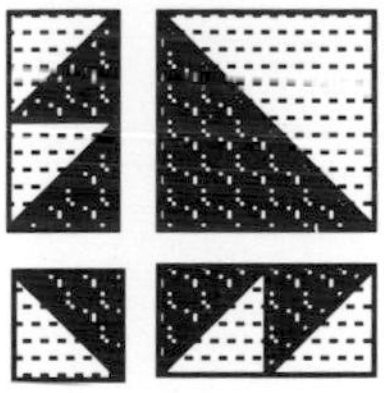

Quick-cutting: Cut all of your quilt-top fabrics (except inside border) cross-grain.
- For 2q: Cut 4⅞" strips. Cut them to make 4⅞" squares. Then cut each square in half diagonally to make triangles.
- For 2n: Cut 12" × 18" pieces.

CONSTRUCTION

1. Sew the light and dark 2q pieces together to make half-square triangles.
2. Mark 2⅞" grids on the light 2n pieces. Pair them up with the dark 2n pieces to make half-square triangles.
3. Sew order: see diagrams.
4. Sawtooth border: Stitch the remaining half-square triangle units to form 4 border strips. Sew the border strips to the quilt top, referring to the instructions for "Pieced Borders" in Chapter 7.
5. Corner blocks: Refer to "Attaching Corner Blocks" in Chapter 7.

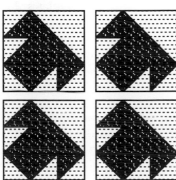

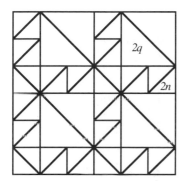

WILD GOOSE CHASE

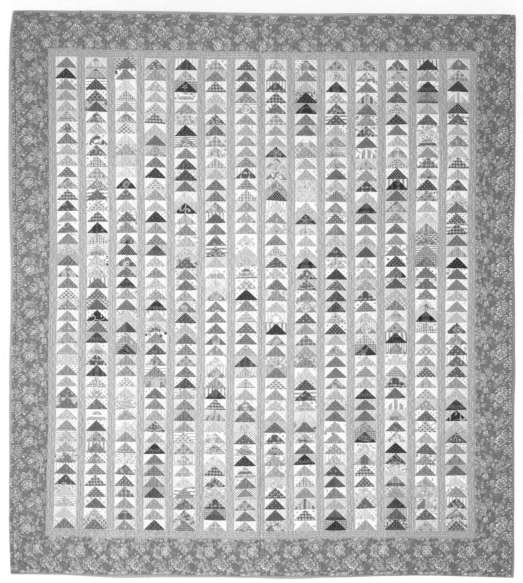

Pat Callis

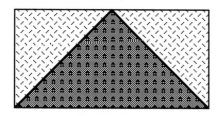

Unit size: 1½″ × 3″

Techniques: Quick-cutting and double half-square triangles or Templates 2m and 6j

Fabric suggestions: Variety of light fabrics for small triangles. Variety of medium to dark fabrics for large triangles. Narrow border-printed fabric for sashing. Fabric for the outside border that complements your finished units.

	Crib/Wall	Twin	Double	Queen	King
Finished size	40″ × 54″	67″ × 88″	81″ × 94″	85″ × 94″	101″ × 94″
Number of rows	8	12	15	16	22
Number of units per row	30	45	48	48	48
Total units	240	540	720	768	1056

YARDAGE

	Crib/Wall	Twin	Double	Queen	King
Small triangle: scraps to total	1⅜	2⅝	3½	3½	5¼
Large triangle: scraps to total	1⅜	3	4	4¼	5¾
Sashing and inside border	1½	2⅛	2¼	2¼	2½
Outside border	1⅞	2¾	3	3	3⅜
Backing and binding	2⅛	5⅜	5½	9	9¼

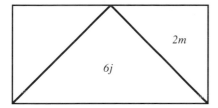

CUTTING

	Crib/Wall	Twin	Double	Queen	King
Template 6j	240	540	720	768	1056
– OR –					
Quick: number of strips	12	26	35	36	51
Template 2m	480	1080	1440	1536	2112
– OR –					
Quick: number of strips	23	52	69	74	101
Sashing strips	7	11	14	15	21
Inside border: width	1½"	1½"	1½"	1½"	1½"
Outside border: width	4"	9½"	10½"	10½"	10½"
Backing: number of lengths	1	2	2	3	3

Quick-cutting: Cut your quilt-top fabrics (except sashing and borders) cross-grain.
- For 6j: Cut 3½"-wide strips. Then cut them to 2" × 3½" rectangles.
- For 2m: Cut 2"-wide strips. Then cut to 2" squares.
- For sashing: Cut your fabric lengthwise into 1½"-wide strips.

CONSTRUCTION

1. Make double half-square triangle units.
2. Sew the units together to form vertical rows. ✳ *Helpful hint:* See the practice exercise for double half-square triangles in Chapter 5.
3. Sew sashing strips between the rows. See instructions for sashing in Chapter 6 for help in keeping the units straight when attaching the sashing strips.

NOTE: For the arrangement shown in the planned *Sampler* quilt on page 9 use Templates 2n and 2r or, for quick methods, cut 2½" squares and 2½" × 4½" rectangles.

WILD GOOSE CHASE VARIATION

Block size: 12″
Techniques: Strip piecing and double half-square triangles or Templates 1e, 2n and 2r
Setting: Straight
Fabric suggestions: Medium color solid fabric for small triangles. Variety of scraps for large triangles. Three different fabrics for strips. Border fabric that complements your finished blocks.

	Crib/Wall	Twin	Double	Queen	King
Finished size	40″×52″	58″×58″	66″×90″	80″×92″	104″×92″
Blocks set	3×4	4×4	4×6	5×6	7×6
Total blocks	12	16	24	30	42

YARDAGE

	Crib/Wall	Twin	Double	Queen	King
Small triangle	1½	2	2¾	3⅜	4⅝
Large triangle: scraps to total	1⅜	1¾	2¾	3⅛	4¼
Strips: three *each* at	⅜	½	½	¾	⅞
Border	1¾	2	3	3	3¼
Backing and binding	2⅛	3½	5⅜	5½	9

CUTTING

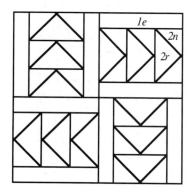

	Crib/Wall	Twin	Double	Queen	King
Template 2n	288	384	576	720	1008
–OR–					
Quick: number of strips	18	24	36	45	63
Template 2r	144	192	288	360	504
–OR–					
Quick: number of strips	9	12	18	23	32
Template 1e	96	128	192	240	336
–OR–					
Quick: number of strips	4	8	11	14	19
Border: width	2½″	5½″	9½″	10½″	10½″
Backing: number of lengths	1	2	2	2	3

Quick-cutting: Cut your quilt-top fabric (except borders) crossgrain.
- For 2n: Cut 2½″-wide strips. Then cut to 2½″ squares.
- For 2r: Cut 4½″-wide strips. Then cut them to make to 2½″×4½″ rectangles.
- For 1e: Cut 6½″-wide strips. Then cut them to make to 1½″×6½″ rectangles.

Diana McClun and Laura Nownes

CONSTRUCTION

1. Make double half-square triangle units from 2n and 2r pieces.
2. Sew order: see diagram.

✷ *Helpful hint:* See the *Wild Goose Chase* variation practice exercise in Chapter 5 for help.

SAWTOOTH STAR

Diana McClun and Laura Nownes

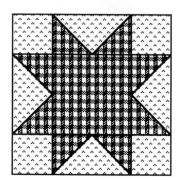

Block size: 6″

Techniques: Quick-cutting and double half-square triangles or Templates 2m, 3b, 4c and 6j

Setting: Straight

Fabric suggestions: Scraps

	Crib/Wall	Twin	Double	Queen	King
Finished size	40″×52″	66″×80″	80″×92″	86″×92″	104″×92″
Blocks set	5×7	9×13	10×12	11×12	14×12
Total blocks	35	117	120	132	168

YARDAGE

	Crib/Wall	Twin	Double	Queen	King
Scraps to total	2¾	7¼	7¼	8½	10¼
Border	2	3	3⅜	3⅜	3¾
Backing and binding	2	5	5½	9	9

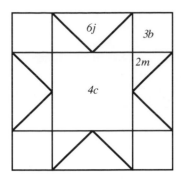

CUTTING

	Crib/Wall	Twin	Double	Queen	King
Templates 3b and 6j, *each*	140	468	480	528	672
– OR –					
Quick: number of strips, *each*	7	23	23	26	32
Template 2m	280	936	960	1056	1344
– OR –					
Quick: number of strips	14	45	46	51	64
Template 4c	35	117	120	132	168
– OR –					
Quick: number of strips	3	10	10	11	14
Border: width	5½″	6½″	10½″	10½″	10½″
Backing: number of lengths	1	2	2	3	3

Quick-cutting: Cut your quilt-top fabrics (except borders) crossgrain.
• For 3b and 2m: Cut 2″-wide strips. Then cut to 2″ squares.
• For 6j: Cut 3½″-wide strips. Then cut to 2″ × 3½″ rectangles.
• For 4c: Cut 3½″-wide strips. Then cut to 3½″ squares.

CONSTRUCTION

1. Make double half-square triangle units.
2. Sew order: see diagram.

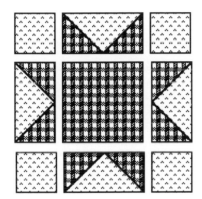

SAWTOOTH STAR

Block size: 4″
Techniques: Quick-cutting and double half-square triangles or Templates 2k, 2m, 3a and 3c
Setting: Straight with sashing
Fabric suggestions: Dark background and scraps for stars

	Crib	Wall	Twin	Double/ Queen	King
Finished size	41″×58″	58″×58″	69″×91″	86″×95″	104″×95″
Blocks set	6×10	10×10	12×17	16×18	20×18
Total blocks	60	100	204	288	360

YARDAGE

	Crib	Wall	Twin	Double/Queen	King
Background, sashing and outside border fabric	3½	4⅜	7¼	9¼	11
Stars and pieced inside border: scraps to total	1⅝	2¼	4¼	5⅝	7
Backing and binding	2¼	3½	5⅜	8⅜	9

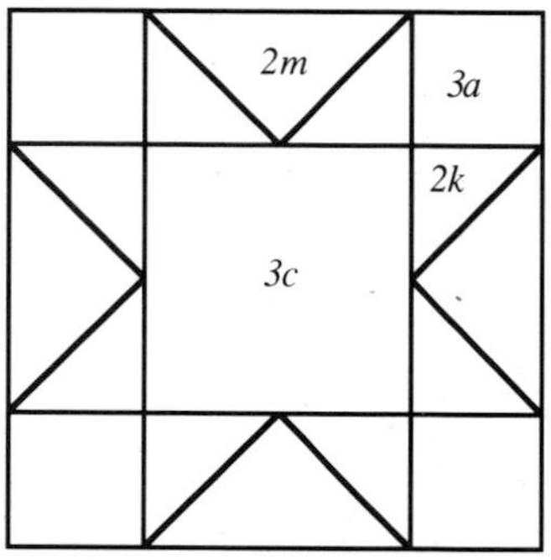

CUTTING

	Crib	Wall	Twin	Double/Queen	King
Background fabric:					
Inside border and horizontal sashing strips	13 *each* 1″×49″	13 *each* 1″×49″	20 *each* 1″×80″	21 *each* 1″×85″	21 *each* 1″×94″
Vertical sashing strips	6 *each* 1″×44″	10 *each* 1″×44″	21 *each* 1″×44″	30 *each* 1″×44″	38 *each* 1″×44″
Templates 2m and 3a, *each*	240	400	816	1152	1440
– OR –					
Quick: number of strips, *each*	9	15	30	42	52
Outside border: width	6″	6″	6″	6″	6″
Star fabric:					
Template 2k	480	800	1632	2304	2880
– OR –					
Quick: number of strips	18	29	59	83	103
Template 3c	60	100	204	288	360
– OR –					
Quick: number of strips	4	7	13	18	23
Pieced inside border: number of strips	18	24	24	30	36
Backing: number of lengths	1	2	2	3	3

Quick-cutting: Cut your fabrics crossgrain except horizontal sashing strips and outside border, which are cut lengthwise.
- For 2k and 3a: Cut 1½″-wide strips. Then cut to 1½″ squares.
- For 2m: Cut 2½″-wide strips. Then cut them to 1½″×2½″ rectangles.
- For 3c: Cut 2½″-wide strips. Then cut them to 2½″ squares.
- For vertical sashing strips: Cut into 4½″ pieces.
- For pieced inside border: After cutting pieces for the stars, cut the remainder of the fabric into strips, varying the cut width from ⅞″ to 1¼″.

Alex Anderson

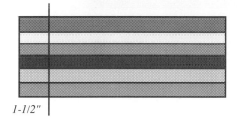

1-1/2"

CONSTRUCTION

For pieced inside border:

1. Randomly sew strips together in units of six. Cut apart every 1½".

2. Sew the cut strips together to measure the required length for each sic of your quilt.

NOTE: Make 4″ stars for the quilt shown on the wall above the bed on page 6.

5″ stars for *Star of Bethlehem* (page 83) border:
- For 2f and 5b: Cut 1¾″-wide strips. Then cut to 1¾″ squares.
- For 8d: Cut 3″-wide strips. Then cut them to 1¾″ × 3″ rectangles.
- For 3d: Cut 3″-wide strips. Then cut to 3″ squares.

12″ star for the planned *Sampler* on page 9:
- For 4c and 2p: Cut 3½″-wide strips. Then cut to 3½″ squares.
- For 6h: Cut 6½″-wide strips. Then cut them to 3½″ × 6½″ rectangles.
- For 3h: Cut 6½″-wide strips. Then cut to 6½″ squares.

ATTIC WINDOWS

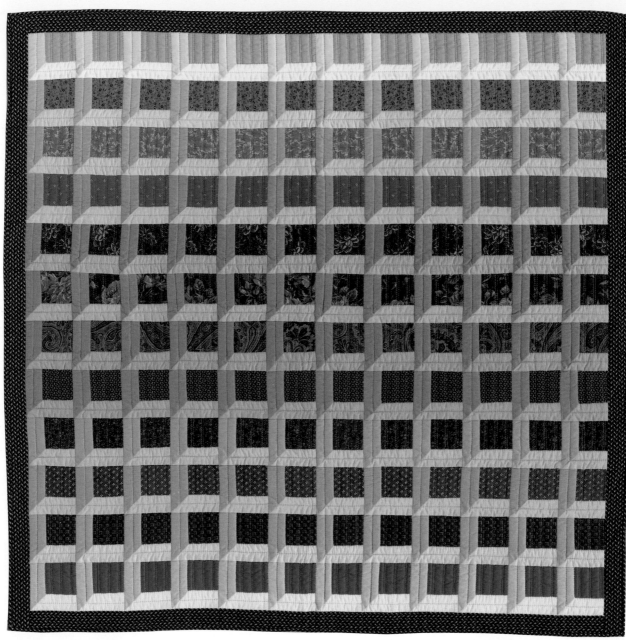

Diana McClun and Laura Nownes

Block size: 12″
Techniques: Quick-cutting or Template 3d, and Template 4f
Setting: Straight
Fabric suggestions: Fabrics graduated in color around the color wheel for window panes. Two shades of each color for the sills and sides. Fabric that complements your finished blocks for the border.

	Crib/Wall	Twin	Double/Queen	King
Finished size	48″×48″	72″×84″	84″×96″	108″×108″
Blocks set	4×4	6×7	7×8	9×9
Total blocks	16	42	56	81

YARDAGE

	Crib/Wall	Twin	Double/Queen	King
Window pane: scraps to total	1⅛	2⅜	3⅛	4⅜
Window sill: scraps to total	1¼	3	3¾	5¼
Window side: scraps to total	1¼	3	3¾	5¼
Border	1¾	2¾	3¼	3⅜
Backing and binding	3⅜	5	8⅝	8⅝

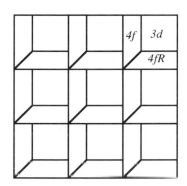

CUTTING

	Crib/Wall	Twin	Double/Queen	King
Template 3d	144	378	504	729
– OR –				
Quick: number of strips	11	27	36	53
Template 4f: sills and sides *	144 and 144R	378 and 378R	504 and 504R	729 and 729R
– OR –				
Quick: number of strips, *each*	18	48	63	92
Border: width	2″	2″	2″	2″
Backing: number of lengths	2	2	3	3

*Note: R = reverse template on fabric.

Quick-cutting: Cut all of your quilt-top fabrics (except borders) crossgrain.
- For 3d: Cut 3″ squares
- For 4f: Cut 2″-wide strips. Then use the template to obtain the correct angle. ☒ *Warning:* Be sure to flip the template over when cutting the sill. *Do not cut multiple layers.*

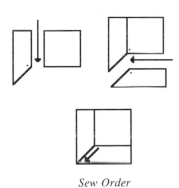

Sew Order

CONSTRUCTION

The technique required to construct this block by machine is called Y-seam construction. You *must not* stitch into the seam allowance at the crook of the Y.
✱ *Helpful hint:* Indicate the stopping point with a dot on the template and the wrong side of each appropriate fabric piece as indicated in the diagram.

Sew order: Stitch in the direction indicated by the arrows.

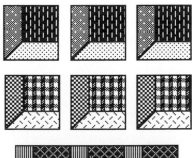

Sew Order

SPOOL

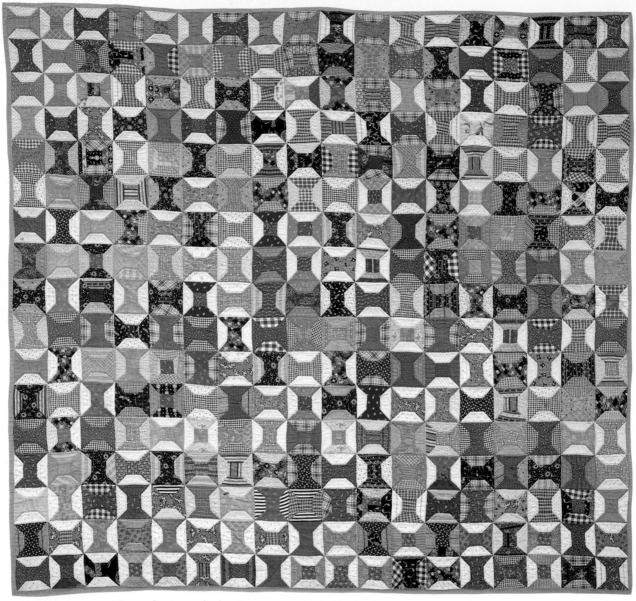

Samantha Ann Wheeler Curtis, c. 1910, Washington State, the great-grandmother of the owner, B. Anderson

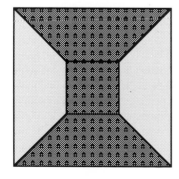

Block size: 6″
Techniques: Quick-cutting or Template 3c, and Template 7d
Setting: Straight
Fabric suggestions: Variety of scraps.

	Crib/Wall	Twin	Double	Queen	King
Finished size	48″×60″	66″×90″	84″×90″	90″×96″	108″×102″
Blocks set	8×10	11×15	14×15	15×16	18×17
Total blocks	80	165	210	240	306

YARDAGE

	Crib/Wall	Twin	Double	Queen	King
Squares: scraps to total	⅝	1	1¼	1⅜	1⅝
Trapezoids: scraps to total	3¼	6	7½	8½	10¾
Backing and binding	3⅞	5½	8⅛	8⅝	9⅝

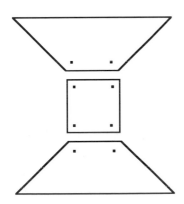

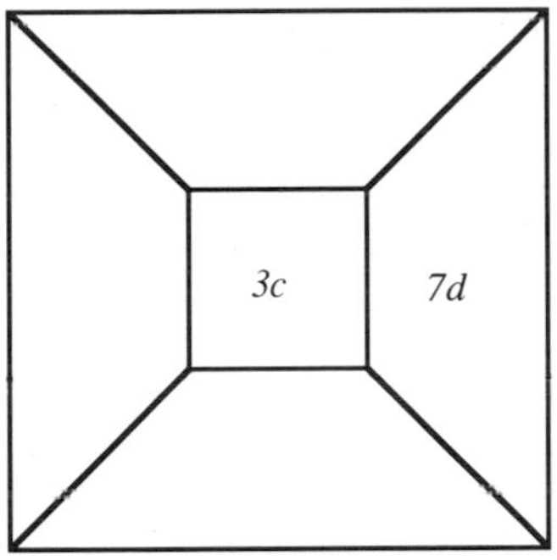

CUTTING

	Crib/Wall	Twin	Double	Queen	King
Template 3c: – OR –	80	165	210	240	306
Quick: number of strips	5	11	14	15	20
Template 7d: – OR –	320	660	840	960	1224
Quick: number of strips	40	83	105	120	153
Backing: number of lengths	2	2	3	3	3

Quick-cutting: Cut all of your quilt top-fabrics crossgrain.
- For 3c: Cut 2½″ squares.
- For 7d: Cut 2½″-wide strips. Then use the template to mark the correct angle for cutting.

CONSTRUCTION

The technique required to construct this block by machine is called Y-seam construction. You *must not* stitch into the seam allowance at the crook of the Y.
✶ *Helpful hint:* Dots to indicate beginning and ending stitching lines are shown on the diagrams.

Sew order: Stitch in the direction indicated by the arrows.

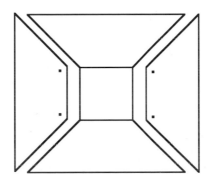

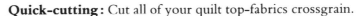

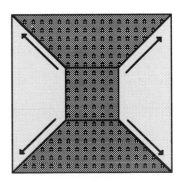

MADISON HOUSE

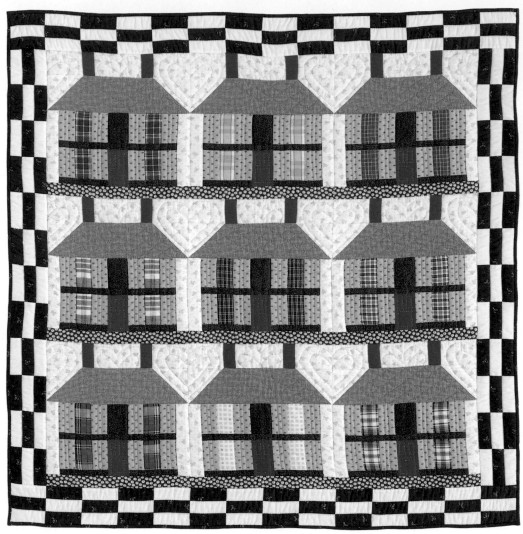

Diana McClun and Laura Nownes

Block size: 12″

Techniques: Quick-cutting or Templates 1a, 1b, 1e, 1g, 1h, 1j, 2p, 4h, 4j, 4k, 5j, 8a and 8f

Setting: Straight

Fabric suggestions: Seven fabrics for the blocks and two for the border.

	Wall	Crib	Twin	Double/Queen	King
Finished size	42″ × 42″	42″ × 54″	66″ × 90″	90″ × 90″	102″ × 102″
Blocks set	3 × 3	3 × 4	5 × 7	7 × 7	8 × 8
Total blocks	9	12	35	49	64

YARDAGE

	Wall	Crib	Twin	Double/Queen	King
Chimneys	¼	¼	¼	½	½

	Wall	Crib	Twin	Double/Queen	King
Windows	½	½	¾	1	1¼
Lower door	¼	¼	⅜	½	¾
Ground	⅜	½	¾	1	1⅜
House front	½	¾	1	1¾	2¼
Sky	¾	1¼	2¾	3	3½
Upper door and balconies	⅜	1	1¼	1⅝	1⅞
Roof	½	½	1¼	2	2⅛
Border, *each* **of two fabrics**	½	⅝	1	1½	1⅝
Backing and binding	2⅝	3⅜	5⅜	8	9

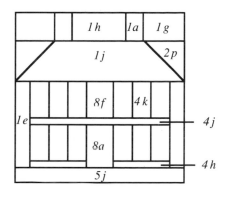

CUTTING

	Wall	Crib	Twin	Double/Queen	King
Chimneys: **Template 1a**	18	24	70	98	128
– OR –					
Quick: **number of strips**	1	1	3	4	5
Windows: **Template 4k**	36	48	140	196	256
– OR –					
Quick: **number of strips**	2	3	7	9	12
Lower door: **Template 8a**	9	12	35	49	64
– OR –					
Quick: **number of strips**	1	1	2	3	4
Ground: Template 5j	9	12	35	49	64
– OR –					
Quick: **number of strips**	1	1	2	2	3
House front: **Template 4k**	72	96	280	392	512
– OR –					
Quick: **number of strips**	4	5	13	18	24
Sky: **Template 1g**	18	24	70	98	128
– OR –					
Quick: **number of strips**	2	2	5	7	8
Template 1h	9	12	35	49	64
– OR –					
Quick: **number of strips**	1	1	3	4	4
Template 1e	18	24	70	98	128
– OR –					
Quick: **number of strips**	1	1	3	4	5
Template 2p	9	12	35	49	64
– OR –					
Quick: **number of strips**	1	2	4	5	7

Upper door:					
Template 8f	9	12	35	49	64
– OR –					
Quick: number of strips	1	1	2	3	4
Lower balconies:					
Template 4h	18	24	70	98	128
– OR –					
Quick: number of strips	1	1	2	3	4
Upper balcony:					
Template 4j	9	12	35	49	64
– OR –					
Quick: number of strips	1	1	1	2	2
Roof: Template 1j	9	12	35	49	64
Border: Template 1b, *each* **fabric**	78	90	150	174	198
– OR –					
Quick: number of strips, *each*	9	9	15	15	18
Backing: number of lengths	2	2	2	3	3

Quick-cutting: Cut all of your quilt-top fabrics crossgrain.

- For chimneys: Cut 2½"-wide strips. Then cut them to make 1½" × 2½" rectangles.
- For windows and house front: Cut 3"-wide strips. Then cut them to make 1⅞" × 3" rectangles.
- For lower door: Cut 3½"-wide strips. Then cut them to make 2¼" × 3½" rectangles.
- For ground: Cut 12½"-wide strips. Then cut them to make 1½" × 12½" rectangles.
- For sky: (Template 1g): Cut 3½"-wide strips. Then cut them to make 2½" × 3½" rectangles.

    (Template 1h): Cut 4½"-wide strips. Then cut them to make 2½" × 4½" rectangles.

    (Template 1e): Cut 6½"-wide strips. Then cut them to make 1½" × 6½" rectangles.

    (Template 2p): Cut 3⅞"-wide strips. Then cut them to make 3⅞" squares. Cut each square in half diagonally.
- For upper door: Cut 3"-wide strips. Then cut them to make 2¼" × 3" rectangles.
- For lower balconies: Cut 4⅝"-wide strips. Then cut them to make 1" × 4⅝" rectangles.
- For upper balcony: Cut 10½"-wide strips. Then cut them to make 1" × 10½" rectangles.
- For border: Cut 1½"-wide strips. Sew the strips to make two different combinations of sets. Cut the sets apart every 3½".

CONSTRUCTION

1. Sew order: See diagram.
2. Sew the border to the quilt top, referring to the instructions for "Pieced Borders" in Chapter 7.

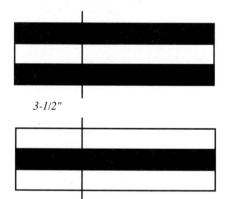

3-1/2"

3-1/2"   Border

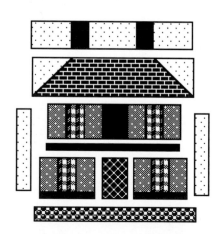

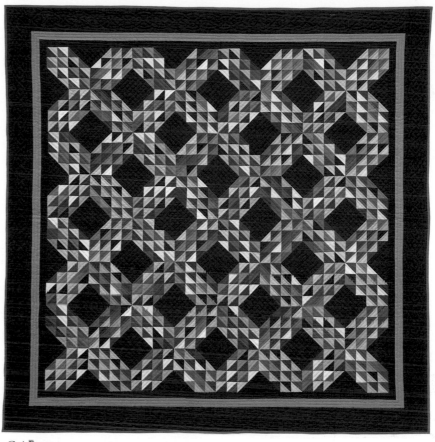

Gai Perry

Block size: 12″
Techniques: Quick-cutting or Templates 3h and 6j
Setting: Diagonal
Fabric suggestions: Dark for background, scraps for triangles.

	Crib/Wall	Twin	Double	Queen	King
Finished size	44″×61″	71″×88″	76″×93″	80″×97″	101″×101″
Blocks set	2×3	3×4	4×5	4×5	5×5
# pieced blocks	7	17	31	31	40
# half pieced blocks	10	14	18	18	20

YARDAGE

	Crib/Wall	Twin	Double	Queen	King
Dark fabric	1	1½	2	2	2¼
Triangles, scraps to total	2	3¾	6	6	7½
Light middle border	2	2¾	3	3	3¼
Dark inside and outside borders	2	2¾	3	3	3¼
Backing and binding	3¾	5¼	5½	6¼	9

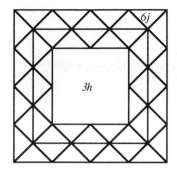

CUTTING

	Crib/Wall	Twin	Double	Queen	King
Dark fabric:					
Template 3h	7	17	31	31	40
– OR –					
Quick: number of strips	2	3	6	6	7
For half blocks: number of strips	2	3	3	3	4
Dark & scrap fabrics:					
Template 6j, *each*	252	612	1116	1116	1440
– OR –					
Quick: strips, *each*	9	22	40	40	52
Inside border: width	1½″	1½″	1½″	1½″	1½″
Middle border: width	2″	2″	2″	2″	2″
Outside border: width	3″	8″	4″	6″	6″
Backing: number of lengths	2	2	2	2	3

NOTE: For quick-cutting and construction instructions, see the next quilt.

OCEAN WAVES

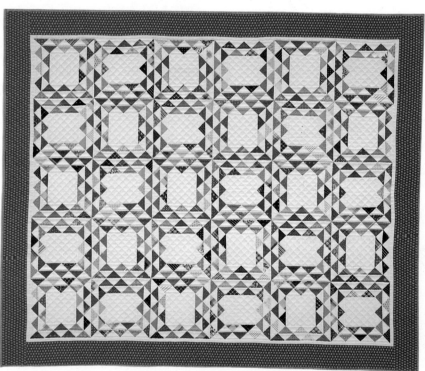

Gai Perry

Block size: 12″
Techniques: Quick-cutting or Templates 3h and 6j
Setting: Straight
Fabric suggestions: Light background and scraps for triangles.

	Crib/Wall	Twin	Double	Queen	King
Finished size	44″×56″	66″×90″	80″×92″	84″×96″	106″×94″
Blocks set	3×4	4×6	5×6	5×6	7×6
Total blocks	12	24	30	30	42

YARDAGE

	Crib/Wall	Twin	Double	Queen	King
Light fabric, includ-ing inside border	2¾	4	4½	4½	5½
Dark triangles: scraps to total	1½	2	2½	2½	3¼
Outside border	2	3	3	3¼	3½
Backing and binding	3⅜	5⅜	6	8½	9¼

CUTTING

	Crib/Wall	Twin	Double	Queen	King
Light fabric:					
Inside border: four *each*	2″×56″	2″×80″	2″×80″	2″×80″	2″×92″
Template 3h	12	48	60	60	84
– OR –					
Quick: number of strips	2	4	5	5	7
Light & scrap fabrics:					
Template 6j, *each*	288	576	720	720	1008
– OR –					
Quick: strips, *each*	14	21	26	26	36
Outside border: width	3″	8″	9″	11″	10″
Backing: number of lengths	2	2	2	3	3

Quick-cutting: Cut all of your quilt-top fabrics (except borders) crossgrain.
- For 3h: Cut 6½″-wide strips. Then cut them to 6½″ squares.
- For 6j: Cut 3″-wide strips. Then cut to 3″ squares. Cut each square in half diagonally.
- For the half blocks (in the diagonal setting only): Cut 6⅞″ squares. Then cut each square in half diagonally.

Step 1

CONSTRUCTION

1. Sew order: see diagrams.
2. Sew order for half blocks (in diagonal setting): see diagram.
3. Assembly: When joining blocks to each other, be certain to match the light triangles of one block to the dark triangles of another.

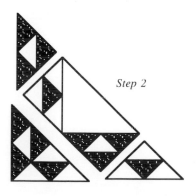

Step 2

ALL STARS

Le Moyne Star, 54-40 or Fight, Swamp Angel, Square and Stars, Variable Star, Memory

Diana McClun and Laura Nownes

Block size: 12″
Technique: Templates
Setting: Straight with vertical sashing
Fabric suggestions: Scraps for pieced blocks. Fabric for borders to complement your finished blocks.
This is an original setting. Yardage is given for one size only.

	Twin/Wall
Finished size	61″ × 90″
Blocks set	2 × 6
Total blocks	12

YARDAGE

	Twin/Wall
Sashing and outside border: two fabrics, *each*	2½
Inside border	2¼
Scraps to total	5
Backing and binding	5½

CUTTING

	Twin/Wall
Sashing : widths	2½″
Inside border : width	3¾″
Inside corner blocks : 4 *each*	3¾″ × 3¾″
Outside border : width	6″
Outside corner blocks : 4 *each*	6″ × 6″
Backing : number of lengths	2

CONSTRUCTION

The technique required to make *Le Moyne Star* by machine is called Y-seam construction. You *must not* stitch into the seam allowance at the crook of the Y. ✴ *Helpful hint :* Indicate stopping points with dots on your templates and on the wrong side of each appropriate fabric piece as indicated in the diagram. Stitch in the direction indicated by the arrows.

1. Memory : for each block
      Template 3c : cut 8
      Template 3f : cut 1
      Template 2n : cut 24
      Template 2r : cut 4
      Template 7h : cut 8 (4 and 4R)
   Sew order : see diagram.

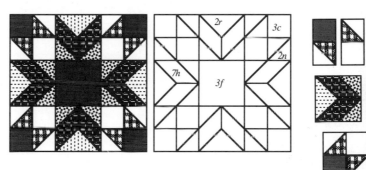

2. 54-40 or Fight : for each block
      Template 3c : cut 20
      Template 6a : cut 8 (4 and 4R)
      Template 6c : cut 4
   Sew order : see diagram.

   NOTE : R = reverse template on fabric.

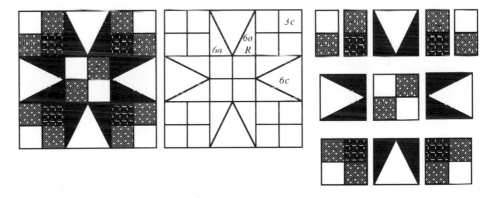

3. Swamp Angel : for each block
      Template 3f : cut 1
      Template 2q : cut 8
      Template 5c : cut 16
   Sew order : see diagram.

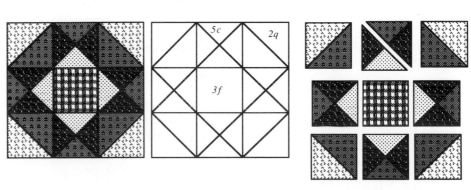

4. Square and Stars: for each block
   Template 2g: cut 4
   Template 4c: cut 4
   Template 2j: cut 1
   Template 6j: cut 24
   Template 2p: cut 4
   Sew order: see diagram.

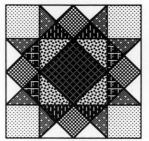
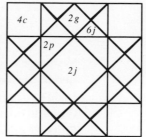

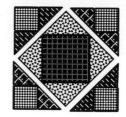

5. Variable Star: for each block
   Template 3f: cut 5
   Template 5c: cut 16
   Sew order: see diagram.

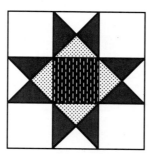
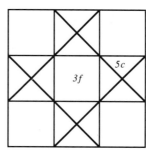

6. Le Moyne Star: for each block
   Template 7g: cut 8
   Template 2h: cut 4
   Template 5d: cut 4
   Sew order: see diagram.

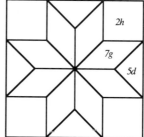
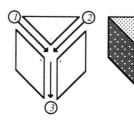

Press the "Y" leg seam open

Press the two "Y" arm seams down toward the diamonds

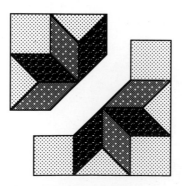

Press final diagonal seam open

PINE TREE

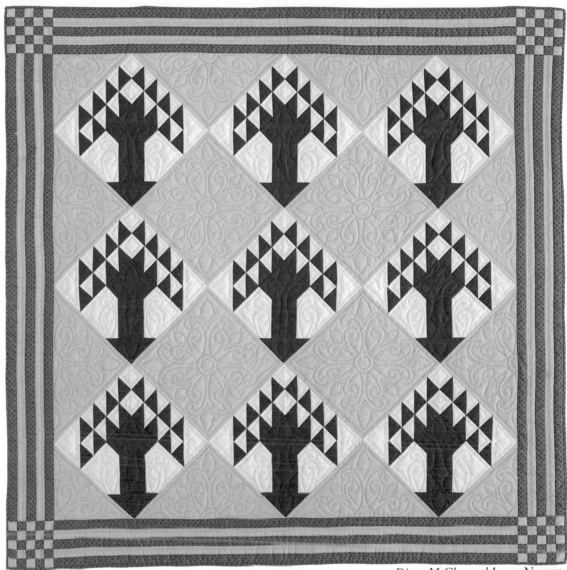

Diana McClun and Laura Nownes

Block size: 12″

Techniques: Quick-cutting and half-square triangles or Templates 2n, 2q, 3c, 8b, 8c, 8g

Setting: Diagonal with alternate blocks

Fabric suggestions: Light for background of pieced blocks. Dark for trees and borders. Medium for alternate blocks, side, corner triangles and border.

	Crib/Wall	Twin	Double	Queen	King
Finished size	61″×61″	71″×88″	78″×95″	82″×99″	99″×99″
Blocks set	3×3	3×4	4×5	4×5	5×5
# pieced blocks	9	12	20	20	25
# alternate blocks	4	6	12	12	16
# side triangles	8	10	14	14	16

YARDAGE

	Crib/Wall	Twin	Double	Queen	King
Light background	1⅜	1⅝	2½	2½	3¼
Dark fabric	2¼	3½	3⅝	4¼	5
Medium fabric	2	3¼	3¾	4	4½
Backing and binding	4	5⅜	5⅝	6	9

CUTTING

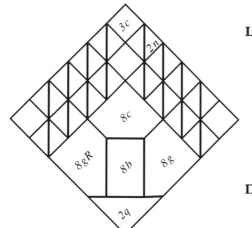

	Crib/Wall	Twin	Double	Queen	King
Light background:					
Template 2n:	144	192	320	320	400
– OR –					
Quick: number of pieces	2	3	4	4	5
Template 3c:	36	48	80	80	100
– OR –					
Quick: number of pieces	3	3	5	5	7
Template 8g*	9 & 9R	12 & 12R	20 & 20R	20 & 20R	25 & 25R
Dark fabric:					
For borders:					
6 for sides A, *each*	1½"×55"	2½"×72"	1½"×89"	2"×89"	2"×89"
6 for sides B, *each*	1½"×55"	2½"×55"	1½"×72"	2"×72"	2"×89"
For corner blocks: five strips, *each*	1½"×22"	2½"×34"	1½"×22"	2"×28"	2"×28"
Template 2n	144	192	320	320	400
– OR –					
Quick: number of pieces	2	3	4	4	5
Template 2q	9	12	20	20	25
– OR –					
Quick: number of strips	1	1	2	2	2
Template 8c	9	12	20	20	25
Template 8b	9	12	20	20	25
– OR –					
Quick: number of strips	1	2	3	3	3
Medium fabric:					
For borders:					
4 for sides A, *each*	1½"×55"	2½"×72"	1½"×89"	2"×89"	2"×89"
4 for sides B, *each*	1½"×55"	2½"×55"	1½"×72"	2"×72"	2"×89"
For corner blocks: five strips, *each*	1½"×22"	2½"×34"	1½"×22"	2"×28"	2"×28"
Alternate blocks: number of pieces	4	6	12	12	16
Side triangles: number of pieces	2	3	4	4	4
Corner triangles: number of pieces	2	2	2	2	2
Backing: number of lengths	2	2	2	2	3

*Note: R = reverse template on fabric.

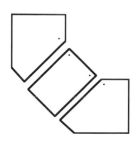

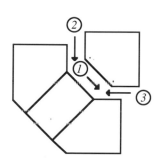

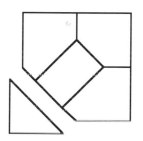

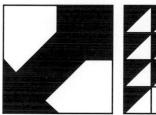

Quick-cutting: Cut all of your quilt-top fabrics (except borders) crossgrain.
- For 2n: Cut 18″ × 22″ pieces.
- For 3c: Cut 2½″-wide strips. Then cut to 2½″ squares.
- For 2q: Cut 4⅞″-wide strips. Then cut to 4⅞″ squares. Cut each square in half diagonally.
- For 8b: Cut 4¾″-wide strips. Then cut them to 3⅜″ × 4¾″ rectangles.
- For alternate blocks: Cut 12½″ squares.
- For side triangles: Cut 19″ squares. Then cut each square into quarters diagonally.
- For corner triangles: Cut 13½″ squares. Then cut each square in half diagonally.

CONSTRUCTION

1. Sew half-square triangle units from the light and dark 2n pieces. For quick method, mark 2⅞″ grids on the light 18″ × 22″ pieces. Pair them up with the dark 18″ × 22″ pieces to make half-square triangles. ✴ *Helpful hint:* Dots to indicate beginning and end of stitching lines are shown in the diagram.

2. Sew order: see diagrams.

BEAR'S PAW

Pieced by the River City Quilt Guild and quilted by Miriam Patsworth

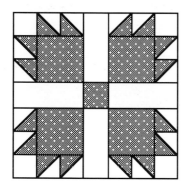

Block size: 12″
Techniques: Strip piecing and half-square triangles or Templates 3e, 4a, 4b, 4d, 4m
Setting: Diagonal with alternate block
Fabric suggestions: Light and dark contrast.

	Crib/Wall	Twin	Double/ Queen	King
Finished size	47″ × 64″	74″ × 81″	81″ × 98″	98″ × 98″
Blocks set	2 × 3	3 × 4	4 × 5	5 × 5
# pieced blocks	6	12	20	25
# alternate blocks	2	6	12	16
# side triangles	6	10	14	16

YARDAGE

	Crib/Wall	Twin	Double/ Queen	King
Light	4	5¾	7½	8
Dark	1⅝	2⅜	3⅜	3¾
Backing and binding	4	5	5¾	8½

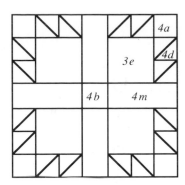

Divide half-square triangle units and arrange in stacks exactly as shown in diagrams

   and

Sew to make:

   and

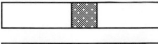

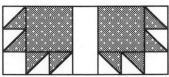

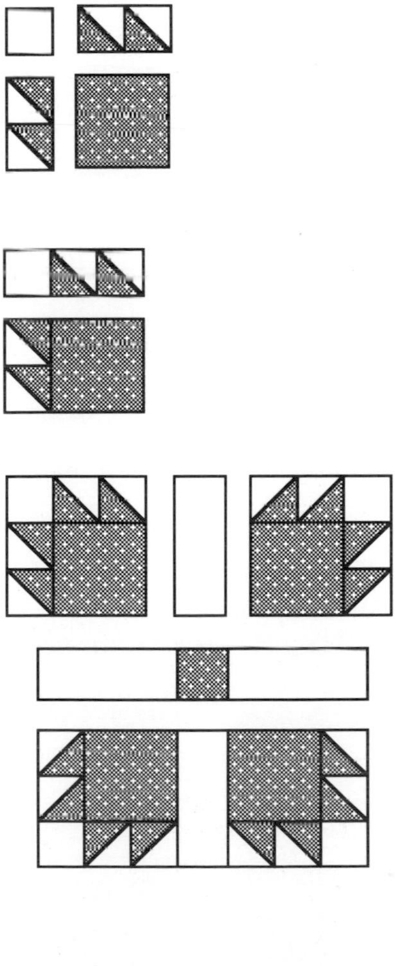

CUTTING

	Crib/Wall	Twin	Double/ Queen	King
Template 4a : light	24	48	80	100
– OR –				
Quick : number of strips	2	3	5	6
Template 4b : dark	6	12	20	25
– OR –				
Quick : number of strips	1	1	2	2
Template 3e : dark	24	48	80	100
– OR –				
Quick : number of strips	2	4	7	9
Template 4m : light	24	48	80	100
– OR –				
Quick : number of strips	2	4	6	7
Template 4d : light and dark, *each*	340	520	732	856
– OR –				
Quick : number of 18″ × 22″ pieces, *each*	4	5	7	8
Alternate blocks : number of 12½″ squares	2	6	12	16
Side triangles : number of 19″ squares	2	3	4	4
Corner triangles : number of 13½″ squares	2	2	2	2
Corner blocks for inside and outside sawtooth borders : 8 squares *each*	1⅞″	1⅞″	1⅞″	1⅞″
Middle plain border : width	3¾″	3¾″	3¾″	3¾″
Backing : number of lengths	2	2	2	3

Quick-cutting : Cut all of your quilt-top fabrics (except borders) crossgrain.
- For 4a : Cut 2⅛″-wide strips. Then cut to 2⅛″ squares.
- For 4b : Cut 2¾″-wide strips. Then cut to 2¾″ squares.
- For 3e : Cut 3¾″-wide strips. Then cut to 3¾″ squares.
- For 4m : Cut 5⅜″-wide strips. Then cut them to make to 2¾″ × 5⅜″ rectangles.
- For 4d : The grid size for making half-square triangles is 2½″.
- For side triangles : Cut each square into quarters diagonally.
- For corner triangles : Cut each square in half diagonally.

CONSTRUCTION

1. Sew order : see diagrams.
2. Sawtooth borders : Stitch the remaining half-square triangle units to form the 8 border strips. Sew the border strips to the quilt top, referring to the instructions for "Pieced Borders" in Chapter 7.
3. Corner blocks : Refer to "Attaching Corner Blocks" in Chapter 7.

KALEIDOSCOPE

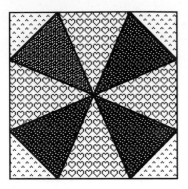

Block size: 6″
Techniques: Quick-cutting or Template 2s, and Template 5a
Setting: Straight
Fabric suggestions: Variety of light fabrics for small triangles. Variety of light, medium and dark fabrics for large triangles. Fabrics for borders that complement your finished blocks.

	Crib/Wall	Twin	Double	Queen	King
Finished size	43″×49″	66″×90″	80″×92″	81″×93″	105″×93″
Blocks set	6×7	8×12	10×12	10×12	14×12
Total blocks	42	96	120	120	168

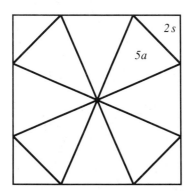

YARDAGE

	Crib/Wall	Twin	Double	Queen	King
Small triangle: scraps to total	⅝	1¼	1⅜	1⅜	2
Large triangle: scraps to total	2½	5¼	5¼	5¼	8¾
Inside border	1¼	2¼	2¼	2¼	2½
Outside border	2	2⅞	3	3	3¼
Backing	3	5⅜	5½	5¾	9¼
Binding	⅜	½	⅝	⅝	¾

CUTTING

	Crib/Wall	Twin	Double	Queen	King
Template 2s:	168	384	480	480	672
— OR —					
Quick: number of strips	6	12	15	15	21
Template 5a	336	768	960	960	1344
Inside border: width	1½″	1½″	1½″	1½″	1½″
Outside border: width	6½″	8½″	9½″	10″	10″
Backing: number of lengths	2	2	2	2	3

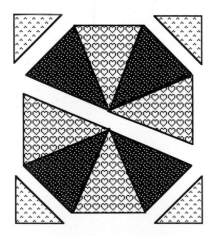

Quick-cutting: Cut all of your quilt-top fabrics (except borders) crossgrain.
 • For 2s: Cut 2⅝″-wide strips. Then cut to 2⅝″ squares. Cut the squares in half diagonally to form triangles.

CONSTRUCTION

Sew order: see diagrams.

THOUSAND PYRAMIDS

Unit 1

Unit 2

Techniques: Templates 6a, 6b, 6c and optional quick-cutting
Fabric suggestions: Scraps

	Crib/Wall	Twin	Double	Queen	King
Finished size	47″×59″	75″×99″	87″×99″	91″×103″	115″×103″
Units set	10×13	17×23	20×23	21×24	27×24
Total units					
One	186	570	675	738	954
Two	61	189	222	246	318

YARDAGE

	Crib/Wall	Twin	Double	Queen	King
Scraps to total	3⅜	7⅞	9¼	10⅛	13⅜
Inside border	2	3	3	3¼	3¼
Outside border	2	3	3	3¼	3¼
Backing and binding	3¾	5⅝	8⅜	9	9

CUTTING

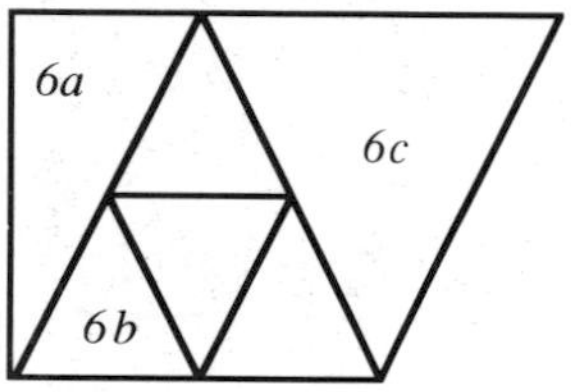

Unit 2

	Crib/Wall	Twin	Double	Queen	King
Templates 6b and 6c, *each*	186	570	675	738	954
Template 6a*	13 & 13R	23 & 23R	26 & 26R	27 & 27R	33 & 33R
Inside border: width	1¾″	1¾″	1¾″	1¾″	1¾″
Outside border: width	2½″	2½″	2½″	2½″	2½″
Backing: number of lengths	2	2	3	3	3

*NOTE: R = reverse template on fabric.

Quick-cutting: Cut all of your quilt-top fabrics (except borders) crossgrain.
 • For 6b: Cut 2¾″-wide strips. Use the template to mark the angles for cutting.
 • For 6c: Cut 1⅞″-wide strips. Use the template to mark the angles for cutting.

CONSTRUCTION

1. Unit Two, sew order: see diagram. Unit Two is placed randomly throughout the quilt.
2. Sew order: see diagram.

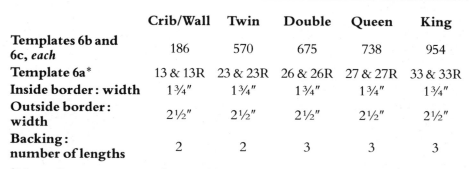

Diana McClun

HEART

Friends of Erin McClun

Block size: 6″
Techniques: Quick-cutting or Template 3h and Appliqué (Template 9b)
Setting: Straight with sashing and posts
Fabric suggestions: Light background and a variety of scraps for hearts. Sashing and border fabrics that complement your finished blocks.

	Crib/Wall	Twin	Double	Queen	King
Finished size	49" × 57"	64" × 79"	79" × 87"	87" × 94"	102" × 94"
Blocks set	5 × 6	7 × 9	9 × 10	10 × 11	12 × 11
Total blocks	30	63	90	110	132

YARDAGE

	Crib/Wall	Twin	Double	Queen	King
Hearts, scraps to total	1	1⅝	2¼	2¾	3¼
Background	1¼	2¼	3	3⅝	4¼
Sashing	¾	1¼	2⅛	2⅝	3⅛
Posts and corner blocks	⅜	½	⅝	¾	¾
Inside border	1⅝	2¼	2⅝	2¾	3
Outside border	1⅞	2½	3	3⅛	3¼
Backing and binding	3¾	5	8¼	8⅞	9⅝

CUTTING

	Crib/Wall	Twin	Double	Queen	King
Template 9b	30	63	90	110	132
Template 3h	30	63	90	110	132
— OR —					
Quick: number of strips	5	11	15	19	22
Sashing width	2"	2"	2"	2"	2"
Posts and corner blocks	42	80	110	132	156
— OR —					
Quick: number of strips	2	4	6	7	8
Inside border: width	2"	2"	2"	2"	2"
Outside border: width	5½"	5½"	5½"	5½"	5½"
Backing: number of lengths	2	2	3	3	3

Quick-cutting: Cut all of your quilt-top fabrics (except borders) crossgrain.
- For 3h: Cut 6½"-wide strips. Then cut them to 6½" squares.
- For posts and corner blocks: Cut 2"-wide strips. Then cut them to 2" squares.

CONSTRUCTION

Appliqué all of the hearts to the background squares using the paper-basted method of appliqué described in Chapter 5.

NOTE: For the arrangement shown in the planned *Sampler* quilt on page 9, use Templates 3f and 9a.

POSTAGE STAMP BASKETS

Block size: 12"

Techniques: Quick-cutting or Templates 2n, 2q and 3c, and Appliqué (Template 6g)

Setting: Straight

Fabric suggestions: Muslin background and a variety of colors for baskets. Muslin for borders.

	Crib/Wall	Twin	Double	Queen	King
Finished size	48"×60"	66"×90"	80"×92"	84"×96"	106"×94"
Blocks set	3×4	4×6	5×6	5×6	7×6
Total blocks	12	24	30	30	42

YARDAGE

	Crib/Wall	Twin	Double	Queen	King
Background	2	3⅝	4½	4½	5
Baskets, scraps to total	1½	2	2¼	2¼	3
Border	2	2⅞	3	5⅜	6⅜
Backing and binding	3½	5⅜	5½	9	9¼

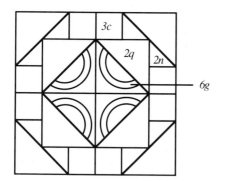

CUTTING

	Crib/Wall	Twin	Double	Queen	King
Background:					
Templates 2q and 3c, *each*	96	192	240	240	336
– OR –					
Quick: number of strips, *each*	6	12	15	15	21
Basket fabric:					
Template 2q	48	96	120	120	168
– OR –					
Quick: number of squares	24	48	60	60	84
Template 2n	96	192	240	240	336
– OR –					
Quick: number of squares	48	96	120	120	168
Template 6g	48	96	120	120	168
Border: width	6½"	9½"	10½"	12½"	11½"
Backing: number of lengths	2	2	2	3	3

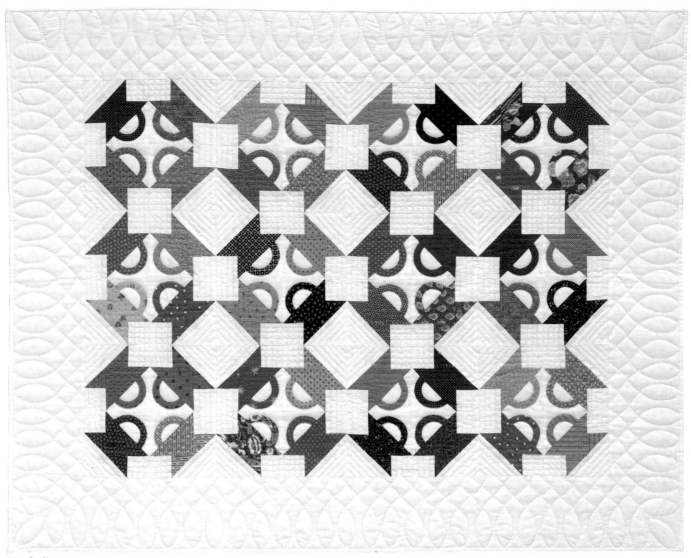

Kandy Petersen

Quick-cutting: Cut all of your quilt-top fabrics (except borders) crossgrain.
  • For 2q: Cut 4⅞″-wide strips. Then cut 4⅞″ squares. Then cut them in half diagonally.
  • For 2n: Cut 2⅞″ squares. Then cut them in half diagonally.
  • For 3c: Cut 2½″-wide strips. Then cut to 2½″ squares.

CONSTRUCTION

1. Center the 6g handle pieces onto the 2q background pieces and appliqué using the paper-basted method described in Chapter 5.

2. Sew order: see diagram.

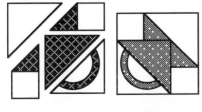

GRANDMOTHER'S FLOWER GARDEN VARIATION

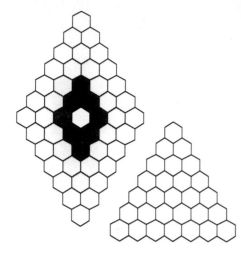

Techniques: Template 1m. NOTE: Use either hand-piecing or paper-basting techniques to construct this pattern.

Fabric suggestions: Scraps for flowers and centers, light background.

	Crib/Wall	Twin	Double	Queen	King
Finished size	38″×51″	57″×89″	67″×89″	86″×101″	105″×101″
Units set	4×4	6×7	7×7	9×8	11×8
Total units	25	72	85	128	158
Total half units	6	10	12	16	20

YARDAGE

	Crib/Wall	Twin	Double	Queen	King
Background	3	7¼	8	11½	14
Flowers, scraps to total	5¾	10	10½	14½	17
Backing	3⅜	5¾	5¾	8⅞	8⅞
Binding (bias)	1¼	1¼	1¼	1¼	1¼

CUTTING

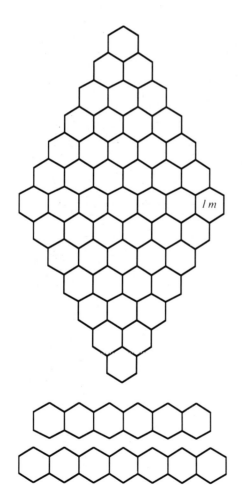

	All sizes
Template 1m for each unit:	
Center	1
Flowers	
Inside color	8
Outside color	16
Background fabric	24
Backing: number of lengths, crib/wall	1
Twin/double	2
Queen/king	3

CONSTRUCTION

1. Sew order for hand piecing: see diagram. ◨ *Warning:* Remember not to stitch into the seam allowance.

— OR —

For paper basting: Cut your 1m paper pattern along the dotted lines of the template pattern. Use a back whipstitch to join your individual 1m parts to each other. In paper basting, you may sew 1m parts together in rows or out from the center.

2. Half-unit sew order: see diagram.

NOTE: For the arrangement shown in the planned *Sampler* on page 9, use Template 1k.

Maker unknown, c. 1930–1940

DRESDEN PLATE

Members of the California Heritage Quilt Project for president Helen Gould

Block size: 12″
Techniques: Appliqué, Templates 3j, 3m, 7a and 7b and optional quick-cutting
Setting: Straight
Fabric suggestions: Light fabric for background and inside border. Sixteen
  fabrics for plates and pieced border.

	Crib/Wall	Twin	Double	Queen	King
Finished size	48″ × 60″	66″ × 90″	78″ × 90″	90″ × 102″	108″ × 108″
Blocks set	3 × 4	4 × 6	5 × 6	6 × 7	8 × 8
Total blocks	12	24	30	42	64

YARDAGE

	Crib/Wall	Twin	Double	Queen	King
Background and inside border	1¾	3¼	3⅞	5⅜	8
Plates, including pieced border, *each* of sixteen	¼	⅜	½	⅝	¾
Center circle of plate	⅜	⅜	⅜	½	½
Backing	3⅞	5½	5½	9⅛	9⅝

CUTTING

	Crib/Wall	Twin	Double	Queen	King
Template 3j: number of *each* plate fabric	20	35	42	56	80
Template 7b	12	24	30	42	64
Template 7a	36	54	60	68	80
Inside border: width	2½″	5½″	5½″	5½″	2½″
Background: number of 12½″ squares	12	24	30	42	64
Backing: number of lengths	2	2	2	3	3

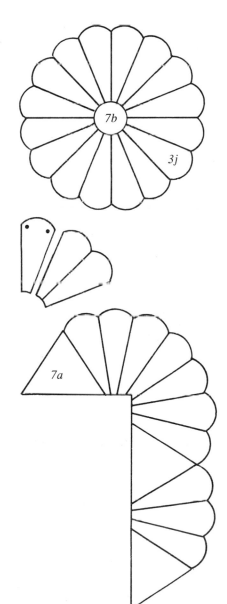

CONSTRUCTION

1. Cut sixteen of Template 3m from plain paper. (These will be used as a guide in achieving accurate curves on the scallop shapes.)

2. Sew order: Sew sixteen scallop shapes together to form a plate. NOTE: Start sewing 1/4″ from the edge of the scallop edge as indicated by the dot in the diagram.

3. Baste a 3m paper pattern to each scallop shape, leaving 1/4″ seam allowance for turning under along each curved edge.

4. Turn the 1/4″ seam allowance under to the wrong side of the scallop shape and baste in place. Press.

5. Center the plate onto the background fabric. Appliqué.

6. Cut away the background fabric from behind the plate and remove the basting stitches and paper patterns.

7. Use the paper-basted method of appliqué to sew the center circles to the plate.

8. Pieced border: see diagram.

NOTE: For the arrangement shown in the planned *Sampler* on page 9 use Templates 7b, 8e and 8h. To achieve the same amount of white space between blocks as shown in the sample quilt, use 14½″ squares of background fabric. Adjust yardage accordingly.

TUMBLING BLOCKS

Diana McClun and Laura Nownes

Techniques: Templates 4e, 6d, 6e and 6f and optional quick-cutting

Fabric suggestions: Three light, three medium and three dark for blocks. One medium for side pieces. Fabric for border that complements your finished blocks.

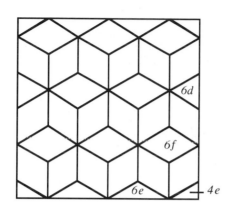

	Crib/Wall	Twin	Double	Queen	King
Finished size	40″×54″	69″×86″	80″×90″	87″×96″	101″×96″
Blocks set	9×15	15×23	17×23	19×25	23×25
Total blocks	128	334	380	463	563

YARDAGE

	Crib/Wall	Twin	Double	Queen	King
Block fabrics: *each* of nine	⅜	¾	⅞	1	1¼
Side fabric	¾	⅞	⅞	1	1⅛
Border	1⅞	2¾	2⅞	3	3¼
Backing and binding	2⅛	5	6	8½	9

Press seam to left

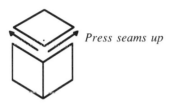

Press seams up

Stitch in the direction of the arrows. Never stitch over a seam.

CUTTING

	Crib/Wall	Twin	Double	Queen	King
Template 6f: **number from** *each* **block fabric**	43	112	127	155	188
— OR —					
Quick: number of strips, *each*	4	10	11	13	16
Side fabric:					
Templates 6d and 6f, *each*	14	22	22	24	24
Template 6e	16	28	32	36	44
Template 4e*	2 and 2R	2 and 2R	2 and 2R	2 and 2R	2 and 2R
Border: width	4½″	8½″	10½″	10½″	10½″
Backing: **number of lengths**	1	2	2	3	3

*Note. R = reverse template on fabric.

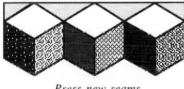

Press new seams

Quick-cutting: Cut all of your quilt-top fabrics (except borders) crossgrain.
 • For 6f: Cut 2¼″-wide strips. Then use the template to mark the correct angle.

CONSTRUCTION

1. Sew order: see diagram.
2. Assembly: see diagram.

NOTE: For the arrangement in the planned *Sampler* quilt shown on page 9, use Template 6f. Turn the raw edges of the outside blocks to the wrong side, 1/4″, pinning in place and then pressing. Center the design onto a 12½″ square of background fabric and pin in place. Hand stitch around the edges using a back whipstitch.

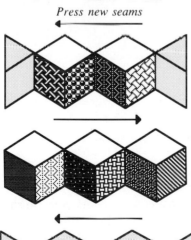

When joining rows, stitch up to the previous stitching line, remove pieces from the machine, flip the seam allowance back and continue stitching.

BASKET

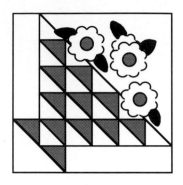

Block size: 12″

Techniques: Quick-cutting or Templates 2n, 2q, 5h and Appliqué (Templates 3k, 5f, 7c, 9c)

Setting: Diagonal with alternate blocks

Fabric suggestions: Pieced block: light background, contrasting fabric for basket, variety of scraps for flowers, with contrasting color for centers, green leaves. Medium color for alternate blocks, side and corner triangles. Border-printed fabric to complement your finished blocks.

	Wall	Crib	Twin	Double/ Queen	King
Finished size	40″×40″	42″×59″	71″×88″	88″×105″	105″×105″
Blocks set	2×2	2×3	3×4	4×5	5×5
# pieced and appliquéd blocks	4	6	12	20	25
# alternate blocks	1	2	6	12	16
# side triangles	4	6	10	14	16

YARDAGE

	Wall	Crib	Twin	Double/ Queen	King
Block fabrics:					
Background	1⅛	1¼	2	3⅜	4¼
Basket	½	½	¾	1	1¼
Alternate blocks, side & corner triangles	1½	1½	2⅜	3¼	3¾
Flowers: scraps to total	⅜	⅜	¾	1⅛	1½
Flower centers	⅛	⅛	¼	¼	⅜
Leaves	⅛	¼	⅜	½	⅝
Border	1¼	1¾	2¼	2¾	2¾
Corner blocks	⅛	¼	⅜	⅜	⅜
Backing and binding	1¾	3½	5⅜	9¼	9¼

CUTTING

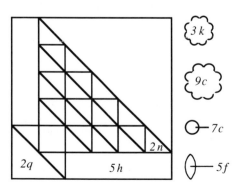

	Wall	Crib	Twin	Double/ Queen	King
Background fabric:					
Template 2n:	60	90	180	300	375
— OR —					
Quick: number of strips	3	4	7	11	14
Template 2q:	4	6	12	20	25
— OR —					
Quick: number of strips	1	1	1	2	2

Diana McClun and Laura Nownes

Quick: number of 10⅞" squares	2	3	6	10	13
Template 5h	8	12	24	40	50
– OR –					
Quick: number of strips	2	3	6	10	13
Basket fabrics:					
Template 2n	48	72	144	240	300
– OR –					
Quick: number of strips	2	3	6	9	11

Alternate blocks: number of 12½″ squares	1	2	6	12	16
Side triangles: number of 19″ squares	1	2	3	4	4
Corner triangles: number of 13½″ squares	2	2	2	2	2
Small flower: Template 3k	4	6	12	20	25
Large flower: Template 9c	12	18	36	60	75
Centers: Template 7c	4	6	12	20	25
Leaves: Template 5f	20	30	60	100	125
Border: width	3½″	4½″	10½″	10½″	10½″
Corner blocks, each square	3½″	4½″	10½″	10½″	10½″
Backing: number of lengths	1	2	2	3	3

Quick-cutting: Cut all of your quilt-top fabrics (except borders) crossgrain.
- For 2n: Cut 2⅞″-wide strips. Then cut to 2⅞″ squares. Cut each square in half diagonally.
- For 2q: Cut 4⅞″-wide strips. Then cut to 4⅞″ squares. Cut each square in half diagonally.
- For 5h: Cut 2½″-wide strips. Then cut them to 2½″ × 8½″ rectangles.
- Cut each 10⅞″ square of background fabric in half diagonally.

CONSTRUCTION

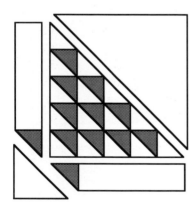

1. Sew order: see diagram.
2. Using the paper-basted method of appliqué from Chapter 5, attach the leaves and flowers.

STAR OF BETHLEHEM

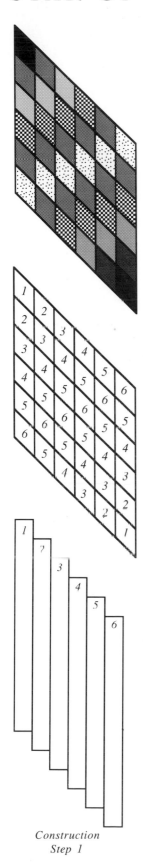

*Construction
Step 1*

Techniques: Strip piecing and double half-square triangles or Templates: crib/wall, 2k, 2m, 3a, 3c, 7e; twin, 2f, 3d, 5b, 7f, 8d; double/queen and king, 2f, 3d, 5b, 7g and 8d.

Fabric suggestions: Six fabrics for stars, one light fabric for background.

	Crib/Wall	Twin	Double/Queen	King
Finished size	50″×50″	70″×70″	85″×85″	100″×100″
Star of Bethlehem size	42″	60″	75″	75″
Border sawtooth star size	4″	5″	5″	5″

YARDAGE

	Crib/Wall	Twin	Double/Queen	King
Color:				
Number one	³⁄₈	¹⁄₂	⁵⁄₈	⁵⁄₈
Number two	¹⁄₂	⁵⁄₈	³⁄₄	³⁄₄
Numbers three and six, *each*	⁵⁄₈	³⁄₄	1	1
Number four	³⁄₄	⁷⁄₈	1 ¹⁄₈	1 ¹⁄₈
Number five	⁷⁄₈	1	1 ³⁄₈	1 ³⁄₈
Background	1 ³⁄₄	2 ³⁄₄	3 ³⁄₈	3 ³⁄₈
Inside border	⁵⁄₈	1 ³⁄₄	2 ¹⁄₄	2 ¹⁄₄
Binding	³⁄₈	¹⁄₂	⁵⁄₈	³⁄₄
Backing	3	4 ¹⁄₄	7 ¹⁄₂	8 ³⁄₄
Outside border (king only)	—	—	—	3 ¹⁄₄

CUTTING

	All sizes
Center star: Use Template 7e, 7f or 7g	
Template — color one	16
— OR —	
Quick: number of strips	2
Template — color two	32
— OR —	
Quick: number of strips	4
Template — colors three and six, *each*	48
— OR —	
Quick: number of strips	6
Template — color four	64
— OR —	
Quick: number of strips	8
Template — color five	80
— OR —	
Quick: number of strips	10

Diana McClun and Laura Nownes

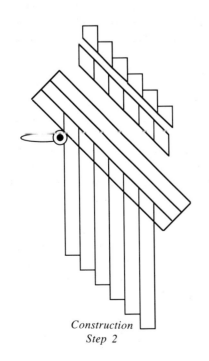

*Construction
Step 2*

	Crib/Wall	Twin	Double/ Queen	King
Background:				
For side triangles, cut one square	19½″×19½″	27″×27″	34″×34″	34″×34″
For corner squares, *each*	14″×14″	18½″×18½″	22″×22″	22″×22″
Inside border: width	1¼″	1¼″	1¼″	1¼″
Pieced star border:				
Template 3a or 2f	96	80	128	128
— *OR* —				
Quick: number of strips	4	4	6	6
Template 2k or 5b	192	160	256	256
— *OR* —				
Quick: number of strips	7	7	11	11
Template 2m or 8d	96	80	128	128
— *OR* —				
Quick: number of strips	4	4	6	6
Template 3c or 3d	24	20	32	32
— *OR* —				
Quick: number of strips	2	2	3	3

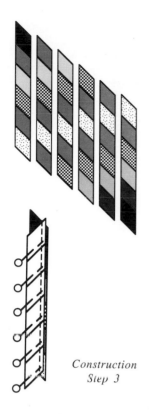

Alternate blocks in border:				
Quick: number of pieces	24	20	32	32
Outside border: width (king only)	—	—	—	8"
Backing: number of lengths	2	2	3	3

Quick-cutting: Cut all of your quilt-top fabrics (except for inside borders for twin, double/queen and king) crossgrain.
- For center *Star of Bethlehem*:
   Crib/Wall—Cut 2"-wide strips.
   Twin—Cut 2½"-wide strips.
   All other sizes—Cut 3"-wide strips.
- For side triangles: Cut the square into quarters diagonally.
- For border stars: See specific cutting instructions for *Sawtooth Star* on page 47. Use the remainder of the 6 star fabrics.
   Crib/Wall—Make twenty-four 4" stars.
   Twin—Make twenty 5" stars.
   All other sizes—Make thirty-two 5" stars.
- For alternate blocks in border:
   Crib/Wall—Cut twenty-four 4½" squares.
   Twin—Cut twenty 5½" × 6½" rectangles.
   All other sizes—Cut thirty-two 5½" squares.

CONSTRUCTION

1. Sew two sets of each of the following combinations, offsetting the strips exactly as shown in the diagram. Press all your seams in each set towards the first strip.

   Combinations: 1-2-3-4-5-6
   2-3-4-5-6-5
   3-4-5-6-5-4

2. Use the 45-degree angle on your wide plastic ruler to measure and then cut diagonal strips either 2", 2½" or 3" wide, depending on your quilt size. ☐ *Warning:* This is a critical step, as these angles can be hard to achieve. Be as accurate as possible: do not rush. You may have to readjust the cut edge after two or three strips.

3. Sew order for *Star of Bethlehem*: see diagram.

4. Assembly: The technique required to construct this pattern by machine is called Y-seam construction. You *must not* stitch into the seam allowance at the crook of the Y. Stitch in the direction of the arrows. The distance from A to B must be the same on each corner and triangle piece. Measure and pin for accuracy before sewing. NOTE: The seams between the assembled diamond units are pressed open. This is one of the few instances in quiltmaking where seams are pressed open rather than to one side. Open seams eliminate bulk and allow the diamond points to join accurately at the center of the star.

5. Make the pieced border strips.

6. Corner squares and side triangles of background fabric are cut slightly too large. Straighten the edges and trim the excess fabric as necessary to allow first the inner border and then the pieced border to fit properly. NOTE: Star sizes vary, you may have more space between the star points and the inner border than as shown in the sample quilt.

*Construction
Step 3*

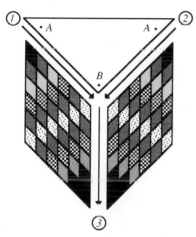

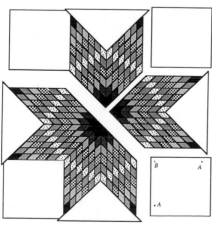

*Construction
Step 4*

DRUNKARD'S PATH

Maker unknown, c. 1910–1930

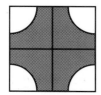

Block One

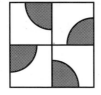

Block Two

Block size: 6″
Techniques: Templates 2p, 5e, 5g and optional quick-cutting, hand piecing
Setting: Straight
Fabric suggestions: Four colors of your choice.

	Crib/Wall	Twin	Double	Queen	King
Finished size	39″×51″	63″×75″	63″×99″	87″×99″	111″×99″
Blocks set	3×5	7×9	7×13	11×13	15×13
Total blocks:					
One	8	32	46	72	98
Two	7	31	45	71	97

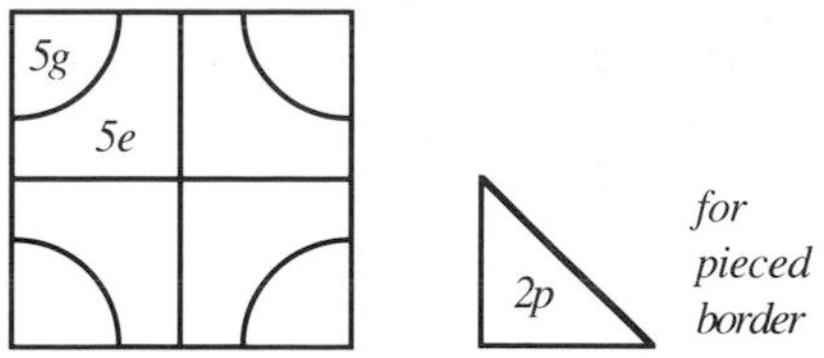

YARDAGE

	Crib/Wall	Twin	Double	Queen	King
Color one (black)	2⅜	4⅛	5⅜	5¾	6⅞
Color two (salmon)	¾	1¼	2	3	4
Color three (blue)	¾	1⅛	1¼	1½	1⅝
Color four (brown)	¾	1⅛	1⅜	1⅝	1¾
Backing and binding	3⅜	4¾	6	9	9

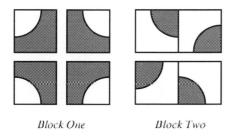

Block One   *Block Two*

CUTTING

	Crib/Wall	Twin	Double	Queen	King
Color one:					
Inside border: four *each*	2″ × 35″	2″ × 59″	2″ × 83″	2″ × 83″	2″ × 91″
Outside border: four *each*	2″ × 51″	2″ × 75″	2″ × 99″	2″ × 99″	2″ × 108″
Template 5e	32	128	184	288	392
– OR –					
Quick: number of strips	3	11	16	24	33
Template 5g	28	124	180	284	388
Template 2p	64	112	132	156	176
Color two:					
Template 5e	28	124	180	284	388
– OR –					
Quick: number of strips	3	11	16	24	33
Template 5g	32	128	184	288	392
Color three:					
Template 5e	64	112	132	156	176
Color four:					
Template 5g	64	112	132	156	176
Backing: number of lengths	2	2	2	3	3

Quick-cutting: Cut all of your fabrics (except borders) crossgrain.
- For 5e: Cut 3½″-wide strips. Then use template to mark curve for cutting.

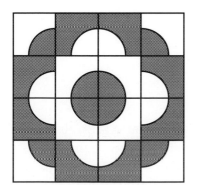

Border Sew Order

CONSTRUCTION

✱ *Helpful hint:* See the *Drunkard's Path* practice exercise in Chapter 5 for help.
1. Block One sew order: see diagram.
2. Block Two sew order: see diagram.
3. Assembly: Alternate Blocks One and Two, starting with Block One in a corner.
4. Border sew order: see diagram.

Setting in the planned Sampler

CHAPTER 3

COLOR SELECTION

Color is magic in quilts. More than pattern or design, it is the one single element that tells us a great deal about the quilt—and the person who made it. We are all aware of the importance and power of color. However, all of us are insecure about our color choices when we project from fabric swatches to an entire quilt. We want the color to fall into place, to make us feel excited and creative. We want the quilt to enhance the environment for which it was intended. We want the choices to say "ME!"

Because of the overwhelming abundance of fabrics available, the selection of color is an extremely difficult task. Do not let any negative thoughts you may have with regard to your ability to choose the "right" colors get in the way of your starting on a quilt—today! We are giving you solid guidelines for choosing a color scheme. Use them to give yourself confidence in developing your own individual style. If you are a beginner, think of this as your "first" quilt and not your "one and only." The important step now is to begin. Trust yourself.

COLOR SCHEMES

MONOCHROMATIC

As the name implies, only one color is used. All the shades, tints and tones which can be made from that color are considered. Just think of all the different greens there are in nature and you can produce a monochromatic color scheme. Take a pair of scissors and go out into your garden or yard. Clip a variety of greenery from the various plants and

grasses. Take these clippings back into the house and lay them out on a white (or light neutral) surface. Study the clippings and you will soon be excited by the variety of tints and tones. If your choice is a mono-chromatic color scheme, this simple exercise can be your guide when you go to buy your fabric. Diana used this exercise to plan her *Thousand Pyramids* quilt on page 69.

ANALOGOUS

This is made by referring to the color wheel and selecting adjacent colors. These colors just naturally go together because they share a color in common. For example, in the use of violet, blue-violet and blue, you can expand the scheme by adding blue-green and green and, for more variety, include the five colors that have blue in common. See Diana and Laura's *Wild Goose Chase* variation quilt on page 43.

COMPLEMENTARY

This uses one color and its complement—red and green, blue and orange, yellow and violet. Opposite colors tend to give brilliance and purity to each other. Together, they attract attention. See Diana and Laura's *Sawtooth Star* quilt on page 44.

PRIMARY

This uses predominantly the primary colors, red, yellow and blue.

The primary colors are spaced at equal distance around the color wheel, so an equilateral triangle can be drawn to connect them. This color scheme is always successful, because you have a warm color (red), a cool color (blue) and a light color (yellow) to give good contrast and sparkle. This color scheme is never dull. See Diana and Laura's *Roman Square* quilt on page 26.

Another triadic (three) color scheme is orange, violet and green. These will also create a lively combination. If orange, violet and green sounds displeasing as a combination, try using peach, lavender and light green.

RAINBOW

This color scheme uses all twelve colors making up the color wheel and sequences them in their natural order as in a spectrum. We associate rainbows with happiness and a fresh new start. See Diana and Laura's *Attic Windows* quilt on page 48.

WARM AND COOL

The color wheel shows the fairly even distribution of warmth and coolness. Most people give more attention to the warm colors because of their dynamic qualities. The warm colors are: red, red-orange, orange (rust and brown), orange-yellow, yellow. These are the colors of the earth and sand. The cool colors are blue, blue-green, violet and their combinations. These are the colors of the sky, water and night. The cool colors have the optical effect of receding in space so that a blue block would seem farther away than a brown one. The warm colors seem closer and larger in size. This is important to the image you want to create. The warm colors also unify shapes and forms placed on them. The cooler colors seem to separate the shapes into more independent units. This gives a crisp, sharp effect. If you want to suggest perspective, combine the warm colors with the receding cool colors. See Mabry Benson's quilt block on page 92.

LIGHT AND DARK

The use of only two colors produces sharp contrast, and the shape and design elements are highly visible. There is no clutter, and the simplicity of the color scheme is always attractive. See the *Bear's Paw* quilt on page 64.

NEUTRAL

Neutrals are mostly naturals: earth, wood, sand, ice, shells, pebbles, straw, bone, ivory, pine cones, wicker, reed. They represent also man-made materials such as concrete, metal and glass. These colors are particularly important to a quilter, because they age with grace. Dirt, fading and aging do not ruin their looks; in fact, they can become enhanced. They are peaceful to view and live with; they do not offend us. They will enhance other colors, so they make marvelous backgrounds. They are classic, dramatic and always correct. See Alex Anderson's quilt on the wall over the bed on page 6.

SCRAP BAG

Choose every and any group of colors from your scrap bag. You can close your eyes, shake a paper bag full of scraps and just pick out twelve or more pieces. Now spread out the scraps and select a single color—preferably one that is missing or an appealing one among the scraps—to unify the parts of the quilt. This method was frequently used with *Grandmother's Flower Garden* scrap quilts, where the flowers often have yellow centers, or a *Log Cabin,* with traditionally red center squares. See the *Grandmother's Flower Garden* variation and Diana and Laura's *Log Cabin* on pages 75 and 30.

TRADITIONAL

In traditional color schemes there is a dominant color, a subordinate color and an accent color. This comes about when you choose a moderately bland color as a dominant one, a slightly brighter color for the secondary support and a much brighter color in small amounts for accent. See Diana and Laura's *Basket* quilt on page 81.

In choosing a color scheme, you need to start with some general idea of what you want your color combination to achieve. The overall mood you want your quilt to have might be soft, romantic, bold, dramatic or sophisticated. Your starting point can be your favorite fabric, a decorative item in your bedroom, a wall or floor covering, a picture from a book or magazine, or an object from nature. An item can help you establish a mood, then a color combination. It is through the analysis of colors in your object, by looking and seeing, that you can be assured your combination will produce the effect you wish to carry over into your quilt.

Here is a practice exercise in observing an object of your choice from which to choose a color scheme. Choose something whose colors you find exciting, like a painting, a flower or a seashell. Write down on a piece of paper exactly what you see.

1. Describe the shape and line (straight lines, curves, sharp angles, etc.).

2. List the colors you see and give a description (light pink, dark blue, dull green, soft yellow, etc.).

3. How much of each color is there?

4. Is there a background color?

5. Look in depth: upside-down, around, underneath, within. Next, assimilate your observations and translate them into fabrics. Consider not only your object's color(s), but also its form, texture and patterning; do not ignore the interplay of these ingredients.

This method of developing a color scheme has worked with success in our basic quilting classes. Once you have selected your fabrics, you can concentrate and enjoy the quiltmaking process rather than worry about the colors; you will be confident that they will work well together. Very often, novices making a quilt will become bored with their fabric selections and yearn to add something new. For this reason, we suggest that you allow yourself enough variety of fabrics.

To help you develop your own color sense, we have asked six quilt-makers with individualistic styles to share their methods of developing a color scheme. Each quilter was given a line drawing of the block pattern *Memory* and asked to develop a color scheme. Since color is both important and personal, you will want to study how others use, see and evaluate their own color choices. But do not be afraid to be original.

MABRY BENSON: Red is my favorite color, so I picked one I particularly liked for the star, then some other reds which went with it. I also wanted boxes outlining the stars when the blocks were joined, so I tried an orange which went well with the reds, but it overpowered them. I made the corner squares all the same blue to form another square. I found a red with just enough orange to add life, and used it in the "arm" of the star. If I were making an entire quilt, I would use a number of different reds for the stars—maybe eight or ten. This would add more variety. ▼

REN BROWN: When examining the block I saw a variety of star interests and enough design spaces to use seven to eight fabrics. The number of fabrics gave me the ability to play with value contrast and highlight the multiple layers of stars which I saw. My first fabric selection was a floral stripe with large and small bands of pattern. Its large dark band became the parallelogram-shaped star points. Using the floral stripe as inspiration, I pulled additional fabrics with a range from light to dark, while looking for geometric prints to complement the floral pattern. ▲

ELINOR PEACE BAILEY: My response to a fabric is always the key to the way I look at color. Being a doll maker, I have great respect for the child within me and her spontaneous reaction. For this block, she instantly chose the yellow and red floral, and the other pieces followed: I held each one next to the mother print and measured my inner response. I used the plaid to foil the sweetness and then I "double dog dared" myself to throw in that outrageous yellow check. The kid said, "Yea!" ▲

KAREN KIMI MATSUMOTO: The large center area afforded a perfect spot for featuring a bold print. I started with the large leaf and then tried various stripes for the parallelogram areas. I picked the gray and black stripe because it enhanced the center leaf. Next I pulled reds to show off the center star. I ultimately used a different red for the outer triangles to create a subtle difference in the star that formed when four blocks are put together. The corner squares were divided into triangles to "soften" the square that formed and so that a series of squares on point, the black floral print, would "dance" across the quilt. The green solid was used to pull the eye from the center leaf. The black and gray print square helps to hold the red triangles together to form strong diagonal lines. The very light triangles were needed to brighten and emphasize the other star formed. ▼

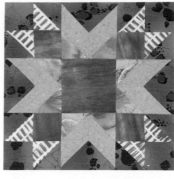

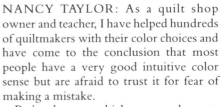

ANN RHODE: Designing provides opportunities to create an interplay of patterns and colors. My main goal for the *Memory* block was to have the star pattern float in space with sections projecting forward to create different planes. I also wanted to use contemporary fabrics instead of calicoes, strong geometric fabrics to contrast with less defined prints, and varied the colors and intensities. ▲

NANCY TAYLOR: As a quilt shop owner and teacher, I have helped hundreds of quiltmakers with their color choices and have come to the conclusion that most people have a very good intuitive color sense but are afraid to trust it for fear of making a mistake.

Red and green, which are complements close in value, tend to vibrate when used together. When their strong intensities play against black—which is even more powerful—the reds and greens glow in contrast to the darkness. It was important for me to vary the scale and value of the red prints in order to create more complexity in the design, but it was also necessary to keep the intensity of the reds strong, so that they would not be overpowered by the black.

When one block design is repeated, unexpected new patterns are created; focal points change, and surprises occur. In the single block, the eye is drawn to the contrast between the central, brightest red star points and the green squares inside them. When four blocks are set together, the green star that is formed becomes very strong and the squares on point that are formed between the stars have an unexpected, transparent quality.

The design unit of the single block is really an incomplete composition; it is only when the units are repeated that the design relationships and pattern possibilities emerge. Then the fun begins! ▼

Selection of fabric for a color scheme takes time, and it is difficult to know which colors should be used and which discarded, but this choice makes the selection YOU. This personal choice is the basis of individual work, and who has the right to say it is lively, good, mediocre or poor? Yes, only YOU.

✴ *Helpful hint:* Now that you have made your color selection, here is a helpful checklist for making your purchases:

1. Is the fabric 100% cotton?

2. Are there any one-way designs (stripes, plaids, etc.)? If so, be sure to purchase extra yardage (5/8 yard minimum) to allow for cutting.

3. Do you have enough variety in color, design and scale? Try to avoid all the same type of design (florals, etc.).

4. Have you chosen a good "ground" fabric? This is a fabric (or fabrics) which will be used as the background of the individual blocks. It is best to use a solid fabric or one which will "read" as a plain fabric, such as a small overall print. Muslin is always an excellent choice.

5. Do the fabrics have an overall appeal? Do you not only *like* the combination, but *love* it? If so, congratulate yourself. This was a big decision, and now you are ready to make your purchases.

After shopping, take your fabric home. Relax. Your next job will be to prepare the fabric for cutting.

## CHAPTER 4

FABRIC PREPARATION

There are three approaches to fabric preparation and the beginning quilter should be aware that this is a subject of much debate. Read through these descriptions; then, make a choice. Whichever you choose, test your fabrics for colorfastness before proceeding to cut and sew.

WAYS TO PREPARE FABRIC

PRE-SHRINKING YOUR FABRIC

Quilters who pre-shrink say they want their fabrics to shrink *before* (not after) the quilt is made.

1. Separate your lights from darks for washing.

2. Unfold *to a single thickness* the fabric you wish to pre-shrink. If you do not and the fabric is not colorfast, you may end up with splotchy fabric.

3. Place the fabric in warm (*not* hot), clear water. *Do not* use detergent. Allow the fabric to absorb the water thoroughly.

4. Look to see if the fabric is bleeding color into the water. If it is, follow Steps 4-6 in "How to Determine If Your Fabric Is Colorfast" below.

5. If the fabric is colorfast, remove it from the water and tumble dry it in your dryer until it is slightly damp. Iron.

PRE-WASHING YOUR FABRIC

Those who pre-wash say this approach not only pre-shrinks the fabric but makes it safer to use. To pre-wash:

1. Follow Steps 1 and 2 above.

2. Place the fabric in warm (*not* hot) water with detergent (or a detergent substitute). Using detergent will reduce chemical irritants and

allergens, but washing also removes chemicals that resist mildew and bacteria. Washed cotton will also lose some of its "body"; it will be softer.

3. Rinse your fabric *at least* four times in clear water. Dry.

4. Check to see if your washed fabric is colorfast. If it is, iron. If it is not, follow Step 6 in "How to Determine If Your Fabric Is Colorfast."

WORKING WITH "NEW" FABRIC

Many quilters like the look and feel of "new" fabrics. They make quilts without pre-shrinking or pre-washing the fabrics, and report no problems. Be aware that your fabric (when it is eventually washed) will shrink *at least* 1½% to 3%. However, it will be more soil resistant and less likely to mildew if left unwashed. Test your fabrics for colorfastness. ▣ *Warning:* If you do not, a fabric may bleed into another when you wash your quilt for the first time.

HOW TO DETERMINE IF YOUR FABRIC IS COLORFAST

1. Cut a 2″ square of each fabric.

2. Immerse one of these swatches into a clear glass of warm water.

3. Check to see if there is any color change in the water. If the water remains clear, then you can proceed. Test the remaining swatches, one at a time.

4. In each case, if the water has changed color, then remove the excess dye by washing the entire piece of fabric in the washing machine (one or two washings) in clear, warm water—*no detergent or soap*.

5. Cut another 2″ swatch of the washed fabric and re-test it in a clear glass of warm water. If there is no color change, proceed to "Straightening Your Fabric."

6. If the water still changes color, you will have to set the dye. To do so, immerse the fabric into a full-strength solution of white vinegar. *Do not dilute it with water.* The amount of vinegar required will depend upon the size of the fabric, approximately 1 gallon of white vinegar for 3 yards. Rinse it thoroughly two to three times in clear, warm water. Re-test in a clear glass of warm water. If there is no color change, dry the fabric completely, iron it and proceed to straighten it. If there is a color change, *do not* use the fabric in your quilt.

Very few fabrics will require this much attention. The ones to be watchful for are the deep red tones, teals and purples.

STRAIGHTENING YOUR FABRIC

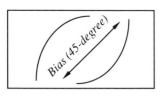

Often the fabric you have purchased is not straight. You can straighten it by pulling gently along the bias. Some quilters find it easier to straighten their fabric after it has been washed or shrunk.

You are now ready to move on to Chapter 5 and begin cutting.

CHAPTER 5

BLOCK CONSTRUCTION

 With knowledge of the following techniques you will be able to make every quilt in this book. Read through them step by step, taking time to practice until you feel comfortable enough to start making your quilt.

Quilts can be made using traditional methods of quiltmaking or with some of the more recent "quick" methods. Traditional methods involve making a pattern (called a template) for each individual part of the quilt block. Template patterns for all the blocks included in this book are given on pages 148 to 156. The template patterns can be used for both hand or machine piecing. You can trace your own templates from them. This will save you the time of having to draft (make an outline of the individual parts on graph paper) your own pattern. We do, however, feel that some knowledge of drafting is important, so two lessons on drafting have been included in this chapter. Take the time to do the drafting practice exercises. This will give you confidence in drafting other patterns which may not be included in this book or possibly designing a quilt block of your own.

General instructions for many quick methods and traditional methods are given in this chapter and marked accordingly. Read through them; then, if you are a novice, do the practice exercises that follow and decide which methods you feel most comfortable with. You may decide to combine traditional methods with quick methods; many quiltmakers do. The practice exercises give detailed instructions for beginners. Although the general instructions will be sufficient for many experienced quiltmakers, any needleworker can benefit from completing the practice exercises, which are filled with useful information.

In Chapter 2 you have seen the many quilts that can be made using this book. Here in Chapter 5 we give the techniques necessary to make them. Once you begin making the quilt of your choice from Chapter 2, the directions for completing that quilt will refer you back here for more specific instructions on techniques.

STRIP PIECING: A TIME-SAVER

The easiest patterns contained in this book are made up only of strips (*Roman Square, Fence Rail* and *Log Cabin*). The width of the strip is determined by the particular pattern (see Chapter 2). The technique required to make these blocks is called "strip piecing." Following the general instructions, a practice exercise for making a 12″ *Fence Rail* block is given. The exercise will guide you through the cutting and sewing of the strips, help you to feel comfortable with your cutting tools and give you confidence to move on to some of the more difficult patterns involving squares and triangles.

QUICK-CUTTING YOUR FABRIC

Cotton fabric varies in width from 42″ to 48″. For purposes of this book, the width of the fabric is referred to as 44″.

Quick-Cutting Non-Directional Fabric

1. Place your fabric on your cutting board. Fold it in half lengthwise with the right side of the fabric facing you and the selvage edges even with each other. Then, fold the fabric in half again, lengthwise, bringing the folded edge even with the selvage edges. There are now four thicknesses.

2. Lay a right-angle triangle on top of the fabric, approximately 1/4″ away from the left-hand edge with the bottom edge of the triangle even with the bottom fold of the fabric. (Note: Left-handed people reverse the placement.) Place the wide plastic ruler against the triangle, perpendicular to the folded edge. If you have a cutting board marked with lines, you can skip this step and line up the fabric with the lines on your board.

3. Remove the triangle and, with the rotary cutter, make a cut along the right edge of the ruler. Hold the cutter straight, not with the blade turned out, otherwise the cut edge will not be straight. Placing the weight of your free hand on the ruler, *push the cutter away from you with one strong motion, placing pressure into the board and keeping the blade tight against the ruler.* This will give a smoothly cut edge. *Do not make short, jerky cuts.*

4. Slide the ruler over to the right, so that the marking for the desired strip width on your ruler is even with the cut edge of the fabric. Run the rotary cutter along the right edge of the ruler, cutting off a strip of fabric. Unfold the strip and check to see that it is straight. ✴ *Helpful hint:* If there should happen to be a bend in the strip where the fabric was folded, you will need to refold your fabric; chances are that your selvage edges were not even to begin with.

Quick-Cutting Directional Fabric

These fabrics will give the best results if cut on the lengthwise grain. You will cut through only one thickness at a time, following the printed pattern, as you will not be able to see if underlying layers are being cut straight along the pattern. It is advised that you purchase no less than 5/8 yard if you are using a directional print. This will give you 22½″ (5/8

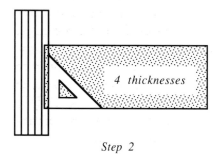

Step 2

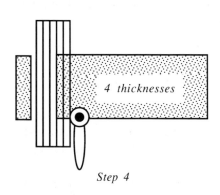

Step 4

yard) along the lengthwise grain.

1. Lay out a single thickness of fabric on your cutting board, with the right side facing up. Using the rotary cutter and wide plastic ruler, cut off the selvage edge.

2. In order to cut an accurate width of fabric, place the desired strip width marking of your ruler even with the cut edge of the fabric.

3. Run your rotary cutter along the edge of the ruler, cutting off a strip of fabric.

4. Continue cutting strips along the lengthwise grain the required width for the pattern you have selected. Be careful to keep the printed pattern straight when cutting. ◨ *Warning:* If you are using 5/8 yard of fabric and the pattern has instructed you to cut four 2″ strips of fabric, you will need to double that (eight strips), since your strips will only be 22½″ long rather than the 44″ strips you have cut from the non-directional fabrics.

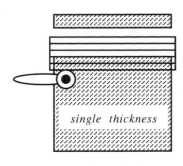

Steps 3-4

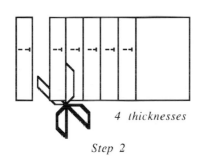

4 thicknesses

Step 2

TRADITIONAL FABRIC CUTTING

Traditional Cutting of Non-Directional Fabric

1. Lay the fabric out on a flat surface. Fold it in half lengthwise with the *wrong* side facing you and the selvage edges even with each other. Then, fold the fabric in half again, lengthwise, bringing the folded edge even with the selvage edges. There are now four thicknesses.

2. Because the left-hand edge may not be straight, using your wide plastic ruler and lead pencil (white, gray or silver for dark fabrics), draw a line perpendicular to the folded edge and just inside the left hand edge. Then, measuring from this line, mark the required width of the strip for the pattern you have selected. Place pins between the marked lines to hold your fabric layers in place. Using your fabric scissors, cut the strip apart on the marked lines, cutting through four thicknesses. ✳ *Helpful hint:* When you are cutting multiple layers, keep your scissors perpendicular to the fabric in order to ensure a straight cut of all layers.

Traditional Cutting of Directional Fabric

This method is done exactly as you did in the quick method, except that you use your scissors rather than a rotary cutter.

THINGS TO KNOW ABOUT YOUR SEWING MACHINE BEFORE BEGINNING TO SEW

In quiltmaking, all sewing is done with a 1/4″ seam allowance. The seam allowance is the distance from the cut edge of the fabric to the line of stitching. *Unless otherwise indicated, we will be using 1/4″ seam allowances throughout this book.*

If you are planning to sew your quilt on the sewing machine, it will be necessary to make an accurate 1/4″ seam on the machine. To determine this distance, place your large C-Thru ruler under the presser foot and measure over 1/4″ to the right. Run a piece of masking tape at this point on the throat plate. ✳ *Helpful hint:* Several thicknesses of tape will prevent your fabric from going beyond that point. On many machines, this

1/4″ is the distance from the needle to the right edge of the presser foot. Also, some machines have adjustable needle positions, allowing you to obtain an accurate 1/4″ seam allowance. If this is the case for your machine, you can simply use the edge of your presser foot as a guide.

Standard throat plates have large holes designed to accommodate needle movement for decorative stitches. When doing small piecework for quilts, fabric can be pushed by the needle into this hole, causing the machine to jam. ✷ *Helpful hint*: If you experience this problem, help is available in the form of a straight-stitch throat plate which has a smaller hole. This can be purchased from your sewing-machine dealer.

SEWING STRIPS TOGETHER

1. Set the stitch length indicator on your machine to 8 to 10 stitches per inch (2.5 on some models). Thread your machine on the top and the bobbin with a cotton thread in a color to blend with your fabrics. A neutral is always good. *It is important to use the same type of thread in both the top and the bobbin to give the best stitches.*

2. Lay out the strips you have made in the required sequence. Sew two strips right sides together along one of the 44″ sides. Be very careful not to pull or stretch the strips while sewing. This may cause them to become wavy. Sew on any remaining strips in the proper sequence.

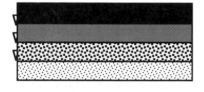

Step 2

PRESSING YOUR PIECED STRIPS

Keep your iron and pressing surface close at hand. Use a well-padded pressing surface, an ironing board or any level surface. A light-colored towel makes especially good padding because it keeps any seam allowance from creating a ridge on the right side of your pieced fabrics. Get in the habit of pressing often while you sew, as good pressing habits can determine the success or failure of construction. This is especially true of machine-pieced blocks. Pressing is important because it maintains flat, smooth blocks and sharp seams. We make a distinction between pressing and ironing. Pressing is an up-and-down motion, whereas ironing involves pushing the iron, which may distort the block size and stretch the pieces out of shape.

Use a steam iron with the heat control set for cotton. The steam setting will apply a little moisture to the fabric and help eliminate any wrinkles. Keep the surface of the iron smooth and clean to avoid soiling the blocks.

After you have sewn a seam, press the fabrics flat to set the stitches in place. Fold the top piece of fabric back, over the stitching line. Press. Seams pressed to one side are stronger than open seams. ✷ *Helpful hint*: If darker fabrics are on top, seams will automatically be turned in the direction of the darker fabric and will not shadow through under the lighter fabric. Make your pressed seams as sharp as possible.

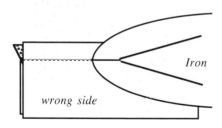

wrong side — Iron

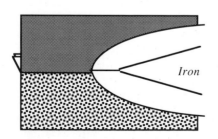

Iron

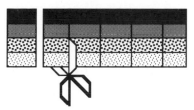

Quick-Cutting

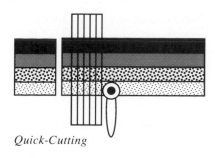

Traditional Cutting

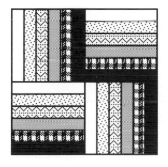

SUPPLIES:
1/4 yd. each of six cotton fabrics
  (graduated from light to dark)
Rotary cutter
Cutting board
Wide plastic ruler and right-angle
  triangle for quick cutting – OR –
Fabric scissors and marking pencil
  for traditional cutting
Sewing machine
Glass-head pins
Thread
Steam iron
Pressing surface
Light-colored towel

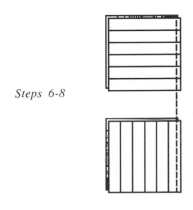

Steps 6-8

CUTTING YOUR PIECED STRIPS

Quick-Cutting

With the right side of the fabric facing up, lay the pressed strips on the cutting board. Using the wide plastic ruler and rotary cutter, cut the strips at the width indicated by your quilt pattern. After a few cuttings you may need to re-align your cut edge with the ruler and board.

Traditional Cutting

Using a lead pencil (white, gray or silver for dark fabrics), mark the desired width on your strips. Using your fabric scissors, cut the strips apart on the marked lines.

With just the above knowledge, a novice can begin quiltmaking. If you are new to quiltmaking, do the following practice exercise.

PRACTICE EXERCISE: Making a 12" *Fence Rail* quilt block

1. Using either the quick or traditional method of cutting described above, cut one 1½" × 44" strip from each of the six fabrics.

2. Lay out the 1½" strips you have made, in sequence, lightest to darkest. With the lightest strip beneath, place the next one on top of it, right sides together. Sew them together along one of the 44" sides. Sew on the remaining strips in the proper sequence, working from light to dark.

3. Press the set of strips. The set should measure 6½" wide; if it does not, check to see that each of your seam allowances is an accurate 1/4".

4. Using either the quick or traditional method of cutting pieced strips, cut the set of strips apart every 6½". Cut four 6½" lengths.

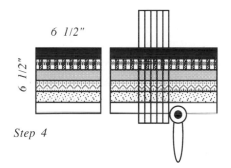

6 1/2"

6 1/2"

Step 4

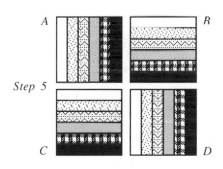

Step 5

A   B
C   D

5. Lay out the four sets of strips (called units) *exactly* as shown in the diagram.

6. Pick up the top pair of units. Place B on top of A, with right sides together.

7. Stitch the two units together along the right edge, making sure the edges are aligned. Hold the two ends together while sewing.

8. Leave this pair of units in the machine and *do not cut the threads*. Pick up the next pair of units and stitch them together as was done in Step 7. This method of sewing units one after another without breaking the thread is called "chaining." It is helpful in keeping the units together and in the proper order during construction and it speeds up the sewing process during piecing.

9. Remove the units from the machine. Notice that the units are held together with the chain of thread. Lay one pair of units on top of the other pair, right sides together. To avoid bulky seams, finger press—that is, push the seams which come together in the center of the near-complete block in opposite directions. Secure with a pin.

10. Stitch the two pairs of units together.

11. With the block folded in half, wrong side out, press this seam. Fold the top half of the block back, over the stitching line. Press.

12. You have successfully completed your first quilt block. It should measure 12½″ square. If not, double-check to see that *all* your seam allowances are an accurate 1/4″.

MAKING HALF-SQUARE TRIANGLES

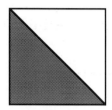

Some quilt patterns will include what we refer to as half-square triangles. These are made up of two triangles from different fabrics sewn together along their longest sides to form a square. This quick-piecing technique was developed by Mary Ellen Hopkins.

1. Using your wide plastic ruler and rotary cutter, cut an 18″ × 22″ piece from each of two fabrics. Cut the pieces as accurately as possible, following the grainline of the fabric. You may need to pull the fabric into shape before cutting, as was described in Chapter 4.

2. Mark a grid of squares on the *wrong* side of the lighter fabric. A grid is a pattern of horizontal and vertical lines forming squares of uniform size. The size of the grid will be 7/8″ larger than the finished size of the half-square triangle. Use your right-angle triangle and a black ultra-fine permanent pen to mark accurate 90-degree angle lines. ◼ *Warning*: Permanent ink pens are used *only* for marking cutting lines on fabric. They are *not* used for marking the stitching lines. Place dots on the lines at intervals of the required size of the grid.

3. Using your wide plastic ruler, connect the dots vertically and horizontally to form the grid.

4. Using a red ultra-fine permanent pen, lightly mark diagonal lines in every other row of the grid as indicated in the diagram.

5. Next, lightly mark diagonal lines going in the opposite direction in all of the empty squares.

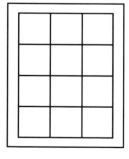

Step 3

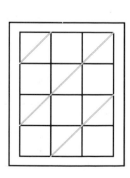

Step 4

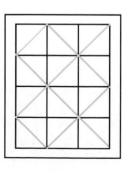

Step 5

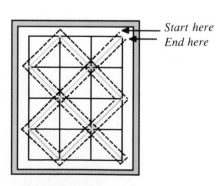

Start here
End here

Step 6

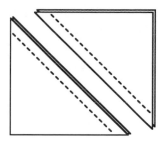

Step 7

Step 8

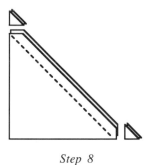

SUPPLIES:
1/2 yd. each of two fabrics (one
light and one dark)
Cutting board
Wide plastic ruler
Rotary cutter or fabric scissors
Ultra-fine permanent pens in black
and red
Plastic right-angle triangle
Glass-head pins
Sewing machine
Thread
Steam iron
Pressing surface
Light-colored towel

6. With their right sides together, place this marked fabric on top of the darker fabric. Lightly press the two layers together to remove any possible wrinkles. Place a few pins to hold the two layers in place. Starting in a corner which has a diagonal line going in towards the center of the grid, begin stitching 1/4″ to the left of the diagonal line, stopping to pivot at the corners and continuing around the grid until you have returned to the beginning. Every diagonal line will now have a 1/4″ stitching line on *both* sides.

7. Remove the pins. Press well. Lay the fabrics on the cutting board. Using your wide plastic ruler and rotary cutter or fabric scissors, cut through both thicknesses of fabric, cutting on *every* marked line (horizontal, vertical and diagonal).

8. Use your scissors or rotary cutter to cut off the corners of the triangles, as pictured. Press the unit flat, then fold the top triangle back over the stitching line. Press, to form a square.

You will discover that each marked square on the grid made two half-square triangles. Therefore, if you have a grid of 4 squares across and 5 squares down (20 squares), you will end up with a total of 40 half-square triangles.

PRACTICE EXERCISE: Making a 12″ *Pinwheel* quilt block

1. Cut a 12″ × 15″ piece from each of the two fabrics.
2. Mark a 2⅛″ grid and diagonals on the wrong side of the lighter fabric as was instructed in Steps 2-5 of the general instructions above.
3. Layer the two fabrics, right sides together. Pin them together.
4. Stitch around the grid as was instructed in Step 6 above.
5. Cut the grid apart; cut off the tips of the triangles, then press as was instructed in Steps 7 and 8 above.
6. You will need a total of 36 squares composed of half-square triangles to make this block. Divide them in half and arrange them in two stacks *exactly* as shown in the diagram.
7. Pick up the top square from each stack. Place B on top of A, with their right sides together. Place them into your machine and sew them together on the right-hand side. Without breaking the thread, pick up the next square from each stack and sew them together in the same manner. Continue with the remainder of the squares until all units are sewn. Remove them from the machine. Cut the threads connecting the units.

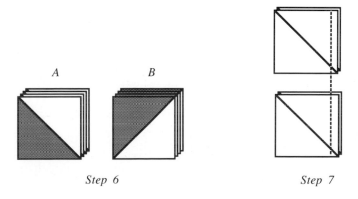

A   *B*

Step 6   *Step 7*

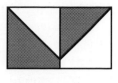

Step 8

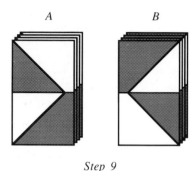

A   *B*

Step 9

press seams

Row 1

press seams

Row 2

press seams

Row 3

Steps 12-13

8. Working with one unit at a time, fold the unit in half, wrong side out, and press it flat. Fold the top half-square triangle back over the stitching line, and press.

9. Divide these units in half and arrange them into stacks *exactly* as shown in the diagram.

10. Pick up the top unit from each stack. Place B on top of A, with their right sides together. Place a pin out of the way of the needle at the seam intersection to keep the seams turned in opposite directions. Sew the two units together on their right-hand side. *Do not break the thread.*

11. Pick up the next two units and sew them together in the same manner. Continue with the remaining units. You will end up with nine units, each composed of four half-square triangles. Cut the threads between these units.

12. Lay the units out *exactly* as shown in the diagram.

13. Sew the three units in Row 1 together and press their seams in one direction.

14. Sew the three units in Row 2 together and press their seams in the direction opposite from Row 1.

15. Sew the three units in Row 3 together and press their seams in the same direction as Row 1.

16. Place Row 1 on top of Row 2 with the right sides together. Place pins at the seam intersections so the seams will remain turned in opposite directions. Sew the two rows together.

17. Add Row 3 to this unit, using the same method of pinning. Sew.

18. Press the seams between the rows on their wrong, then right, side.
✷ *Helpful hint:* Dipping your finger in a cup of water and lightly wetting the seam on the right side helps to flatten any areas that have two or more seams at one junction. This will help remove any wrinkles which may have occurred during piecing. Be extremely careful of the outside edges of the block. Just *press* them—*do not iron.*

19. The block is complete and should measure 12½″ square.

MAKING DOUBLE HALF-SQUARE TRIANGLES

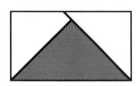

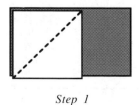

Step 1

There are several methods for sewing these three triangles together, but we like this one, since it does not involve cutting any triangles, but only squares and rectangles. It is also easier for the beginner to keep the finished unit straight, especially when working with smaller blocks. Each pattern in Chapter 2 that requires them will instruct you as to the cut size of the squares and rectangles. For purposes of these directions, no specific measurements will be used.

1. With the right sides of the fabrics together, place one square piece on top of the rectangular piece. Stitch through both thicknesses diagonally across the square as shown. Be very careful to stitch from point to point in order to keep the angle sharp. ✷ *Helpful hint:* If you have difficulty sewing straight across the diagonal of the square, you can lightly press the square in half diagonally and then stitch along the fold,

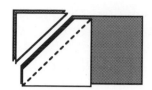

Step 2

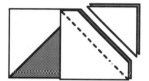

Step 3

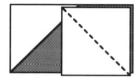

Step 4

SUPPLIES:
1/4 yard each of three fabrics (one dark, one medium and one light)
Rotary cutter or fabric scissors
Wide plastic ruler
Cutting board
Sewing machine
Thread
Steam iron
Pressing surface
Light-colored towel

or lightly mark the diagonal with a pencil and then stitch along the marked line.

2. Using your rotary cutter, trim the excess fabric to within 1/4″ of the stitching line.

3. Fold the resulting triangle over the stitching line and press. Take another square and place it on top of this unit as shown, then stitch across it diagonally.

4. Trim off the excess fabric to within 1/4″ of the stitching line. Then proceed to fold and press as in Step 3. This completes the double half-square triangle unit.

To apply this quick technique to patterns which do not appear in this book, you must know the *finished* size of one unit. If you are unsure, draft the quilt pattern on graph paper and measure the length and width of one of its double half-square triangle units.

For the small triangles, cut squares the *finished* width of one unit *plus* 1/2″. For the large triangle, cut a rectangle the *finished* width of the unit *plus* 1/2″ × the *finished* length of the unit *plus* 1/2″.

PRACTICE EXERCISE: Making a 12″ *Wild Goose Chase* variation quilt block

1. Using quick or traditional cutting techniques, cut:
   • One 4½″ × 44″ strip of dark fabric. Then cut the strip apart every 2½″ to make 2½″ × 4½″ rectangles.
   • One 2½″ × 44″ strip of light fabric. Then cut the strip apart every 2½″ to make 2½″ squares.
   • Two 1½″ × 44″ strips of medium fabric. Then cut the strips apart every 6½″ to make 1½″ × 6½″ rectangles.

2. Following the general instructions above, lay the light squares on top of the dark rectangles to make the double half-square triangle units. You will need a total of twelve units.

3. Lay two units side by side, *exactly* as shown in the diagram.

4. Pick up B and place it on top of A, right sides together.

5. Stitch them together along the right-hand side, stitching just to the right side of the point on the top unit to avoid cutting off the tip of the large triangle.

6. Add another unit to this pair in the same manner. This will make a set of three units.

7. Make three more sets of three units each for a total of four sets.

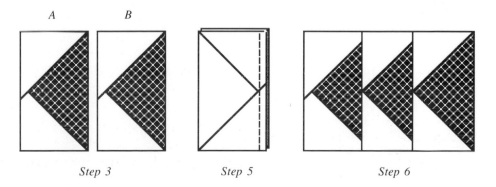

A   *B*

Step 3   *Step 5*   *Step 6*

Step 8

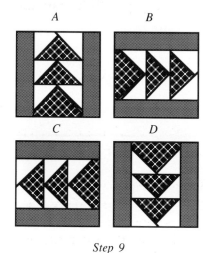

Step 9

8. Sew a 1½" × 6½" medium fabric strip to each side of each set. Make sure that these strips line up exactly with the top and bottom of the sets.

9. Lay out the four sets, *exactly* as shown in the diagram.

10. Pick up the top two sets, place B on top of A, right sides together, and stitch along the right-hand side. Press the seam to one direction.

11. Pick up D and place it on top of C and stitch them together in the same manner. Press the seams in the opposite direction from that in Step 10.

12. Lay the two pairs of sets right sides together, placing a pin at the intersection of the seams to hold them in opposite directions. Sew the pairs together.

13. With the resulting block folded in half, wrong side out, press. Fold the top half of the block back over the stitching line, and press.

14. Your block is complete. It should measure 12½" square. If it does not, check your seam allowances. Remember: all of them should measure 1/4".

✱ *Helpful hint:* If the placement of the dark and light fabrics is reversed, these units can be used to make a *Sawtooth Star.*

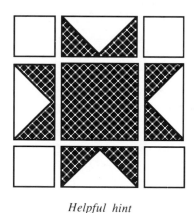

Helpful hint

DRAFTING PATTERNS MADE EASY

Any quilt pattern can be drafted (an outline made of the shapes in the block) onto a piece of graph paper. Once the pattern has been drafted, you can make individual pattern parts (called templates) from template plastic. Although we give template patterns for all the blocks included in this book, we feel that a lesson in drafting is good experience. It will give you confidence to reproduce other patterns and design your own. And it will give you the freedom to create pattern blocks in this book in sizes other than 12" square. Do the practice exercises below and draft the patterns called *54-40 or Fight* and *Le Moyne Star.*

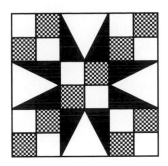

SUPPLIES:
Lead pencils, #2.5 or #3
Ultra-fine permanent pen, red
C-Thru plastic 2″ × 18″ ruler (B-85)
Graph paper, 1/8″ grid
☑ *Warning:* **Check the accuracy of the graph paper using the C-Thru ruler.**

PRACTICE EXERCISE: Drafting *54-40 or Fight* as a 12″ quilt block

1. Using your C-Thru ruler and lead pencil, mark a 12″ square on the graph paper.

2. Place a dot every 4″ around the edge of the block. Refer to the diagram and label these points A through H.

3. Mark the following lines (making nine 4″ squares):

    A to F   H to C
    B to E   G to D.

4. Next, mark lines in the four corner squares and the center square, dividing them in half to make four 2″ squares in each.

5. Mark the points J, K, L and M on the graph paper, then draw the following lines:

    A to J   C to K   E to L   G to M
    B to J   D to K   F to L   H to M.

6. Place a heavy dot at points A, B, J, H, G and M. These dots will be needed in the construction of the block.

There are three different template patterns in this block: #1 (2″ squares); #2 (small triangles); #3 (large triangles). Mark these numbers and the direction of the lengthwise grain on the template patterns onto the graph paper.

7. Mark a 1/4″ line for the seam allowance around the outside of each of the three template patterns. For accuracy, place the large C-Thru ruler over the graph paper, lining up the 1/4″ mark on the ruler directly over the outline of the template pattern, so that 1/4″ of the ruler extends beyond its marked line. Mark along the edge of the ruler with your red ultra-fine permanent pen.

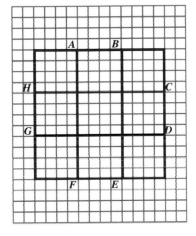

Step 3

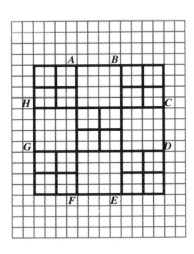

Step 4

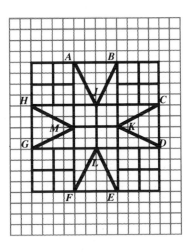

Step 5

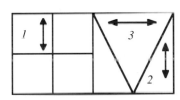

Step 6

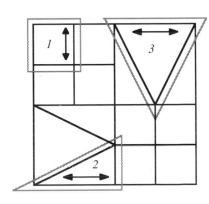

Step 7

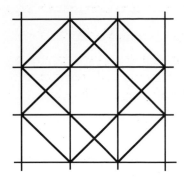

Swamp Angel

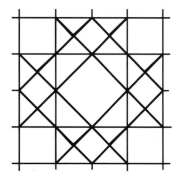

Square and Stars

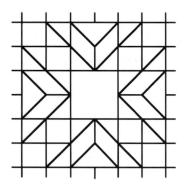

Memory

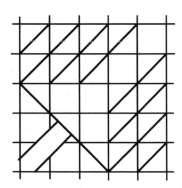

Pine Tree

Drafting can become easier if you will learn to examine the block and break it down into smaller divisions. Count the number of divisions across the top of the block and multiply that number by itself to determine the total number of squares in the block. This is called the grid and it can now be transferred onto a piece of graph paper.

Review the sample blocks below to see how they have been divided. *Once you understand the concept, you will be able to draft patterns for any size finished block.* Divide the number of divisions across the top of the block into the desired finished size of the block to determine the measurement of each division. Each division can represent any measurement. You may want to make the finished size of your block a little larger or smaller than you originally planned, to avoid working with difficult fractions.

Samples:

Swamp Angel. There are three divisions across the top of this block and a total of nine squares. If each division is 4″, the finished block will measure 12″.

Square and Stars. There are four divisions across the top of this block and a total of sixteen squares. If each division is 3″, the finished block will measure 12″.

Memory. There are six divisions across the top of this block and a total of thirty-six squares. If each division is 2″, the finished block will measure 12″.

Pine Tree. There are five divisions across the top of this block and a total of twenty-five squares. If each division is 2½″, the finished block will measure 12½″. (Note that 5 does not divide into 12 evenly; therefore, the finished size is a little larger.)

SUPPLIES:
Graph paper
Lead pencil
Large C-Thru ruler or drafting
  compass
Eraser
Red ultra-fine permanent pen

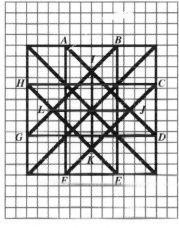

Steps 6-8

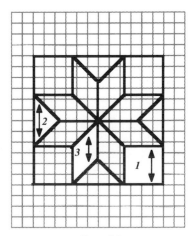

Step 10

PRACTICE EXERCISE: Drafting *Le Moyne Star* (also called *Eight-Pointed Star*)

This block differs from the others because it cannot be broken down into squares. It is constructed from diagonal lines which radiate from the center. Below are instructions for drafting this star into a 12″ block.

1. Using the pencil, mark a 12″ square on the graph paper.
2. Mark diagonal lines through the square.
3. Use the ruler or compass to determine the measurement from the center point of the square to the right-hand corner.

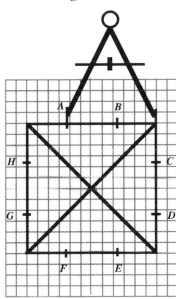

Steps 4-5

4. Use this measurement to mark the distance from the right-hand corner to points A and D.
5. Using the same measurement, continue in the same manner with the remaining three corners to mark in points B, C, E, F, G and H.
6. Mark the following lines:

A to D   A to F
B to G   B to E
C to F   C to H
E to H   D to G.

7. Mark in points I, J, K and L.
8. Mark lines from I to K and J to L.
9. Use the eraser to eliminate the lines running through the corner squares and the diamonds.
10. There are three template patterns: #1 (squares), #2 (triangles) and #3 (diamonds). Mark these numbers and the direction of the lengthwise grain on the patterns on the graph paper.
11. Mark a 1/4″ line for the seam allowance around the outside of each of the three template patterns. For accuracy, place the large C-Thru ruler over the graph paper, lining up the 1/4″ mark on the ruler directly over the outline of the template pattern, so that 1/4″ of the ruler extends beyond the marked line. Mark along the edge of the ruler with your red ultra-fine permanent pen.

TEMPLATES AND THEIR USES— EVERYTHING YOU NEED TO KNOW

This section contains a series of practice exercises about templates: making templates, marking and cutting fabric using templates, and block construction. The instructions given are specifically for *54-40 or Fight*. No general instructions are given for these techniques. If you are already familiar with them, move on to "Hand Piecing: Precision is the Name of the Game." ◪ *Warning:* We strongly recommend that all beginners work through the following practice exercises.

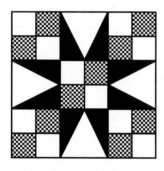

SUPPLIES:
Accurately drafted pattern
Template plastic
Wide plastic ruler
Rotary cutter
Cutting board
Black ultra-fine permanent pen
Large C-Thru ruler
Drafting tape

PRACTICE EXERCISE: Making templates for *54-40 or Fight*

1. Place the drafted pattern on your cutting board. Lay a piece of template plastic over the pattern and tape it in place around the edges.

2. Some template plastic can be scored (lightly cut through the surface only) and then folded to separate. If you are able to obtain such plastic, proceed as follows: Place your wide plastic ruler on top of the template plastic with the edge of the ruler directly over one of the red cutting lines made on the drafted pattern. Use your rotary cutter to score the plastic on this line. Continue in the same manner around the other sides of this particular template pattern. Remove the template plastic from the graph paper. Fold the plastic on the scored lines to break off the individual template. Repeat for the other two template patterns.

3. If you are not able to obtain the template plastic described above, proceed as follows: With the template plastic placed over the drafted pattern, use the permanent pen and large C-Thru ruler to mark the three template patterns on the template plastic, following the red lines. Remove the graph paper from under the template plastic. Place the template plastic on the cutting board and tape it in place. Lay the edge of the wide plastic ruler directly over the marked line on the plastic. Use the rotary cutter to cut the templates apart, cutting just inside the line.

4. Lay the cut templates on top of the drafted pattern to see that they are accurate and that *the seam allowance has been added to all sides*. Also, be certain to mark the heavy dots on the triangular templates.

5. Use the permanent pen to write on each template:
> Block: *54-40 or Fight*
> Template #: 1, 2 or 3
> Block size: 12"
> Direction of lengthwise grain

Now that you have made the templates, move on to the next exercise in marking and cutting your fabric.

SUPPLIES:
1/4 yd. each of three fabrics (one light, one medium and one dark)
Plastic templates
Sharp lead pencil (white, gray, or silver for dark fabric)
Fabric scissors
Ultra-fine sandpaper

Template #2
shown
reversed

Step 1

PRACTICE EXERCISE: Marking and cutting fabric using templates (for *54-40 or Fight*)

1. With the wrong side facing up, place a single thickness of fabric on top of the rough side of the sandpaper. Lay the plastic template on top of the fabric, making sure the lengthwise marking on the template corresponds to the lengthwise grain of the fabric. Using a pencil, mark around the template. Do not press so hard as to push the true size of the template pattern out of shape. If you are using a *non-directional* fabric, you can cut up to four thicknesses simultaneously. Make sure the fabric has a smooth surface and the selvages are even. The folds need to be kept in place with either a light pressing or a few pins. If you are using a *directional* printed fabric, you will not be able to see how the layers underneath are being cut, so you will want to cut a single thickness.

Cut the following for your practice block:
• Light fabric—cut ten of template #1 and four of template #3.
• Medium fabric—cut ten of template #1.
• Dark fabric—cut eight of template #2 (four right side up and four wrong side up, so they will be mirror images).

2. If you are cutting just one thickness of fabric, use sharp scissors and take long cutting strokes. If you are cutting multiple layers and using scissors, pin the fabrics together inside the outline of the template pattern to keep the layers united and prevent them from slipping.

3. Transfer the heavy dots from the templates onto the wrong sides of the triangular fabric pieces.

Now that your fabric pieces are cut, move on to construct your *54-40 or Fight* block.

SUPPLIES:
Fabric pieces
Sewing machine or hand-sewing needle
Thread

Unit A   *Unit B*

PRACTICE EXERCISE: Sew order for constructing quilt blocks (using *54-40 or Fight*)

This method of construction is an organized way of sewing the quilt block, unit by unit. *54-40 or Fight* has two units. Unit A is a combination of template #1, two light and two medium squares. You need to make five of these units. Unit B is a combination of templates #2 and #3, one light and two dark triangles. You need to make four of these units. Organize your fabrics by units in preparation for sewing.

✳ *Helpful hint:* When you are pinning two fabric pieces together in preparation for sewing, the space between the pins should be flat. If it is not, sew with the fuller piece on the bottom, especially if one piece has a bias edge. This will allow the fullness to ease in and prevent the bias edge from stretching while being sewn. You can use the point of your scissors or the tip of a seam ripper to guide the fabric under the presser foot of the machine. Remember that in fabric manipulation you are in charge and the end result should be smooth and flat. The outside edge of the block must be even. *Do not* allow one piece to extend out beyond another.

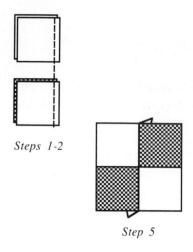

Steps 1-2

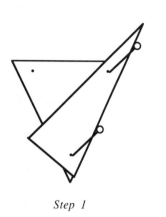

Step 5

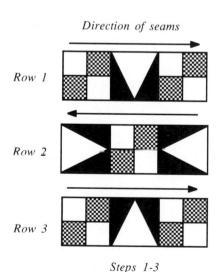

Step 1

Direction of seams

Row 1

Row 2

Row 3

Steps 1-3

Constructing Unit A

1. Place a medium square on top of a light square with the right sides together and sew them together. Leave this unit in the sewing machine and do not break the thread.

2. Next, place a light square on top of a medium square and stitch them together. The resulting unit will be right behind the first unit you sewed together. They will be held together with the chain of thread.

3. Repeat Steps 1 and 2, alternating until all of the squares have been sewn together.

4. Remove the chain of fabrics from the machine and cut the chain of thread apart between every *pair* of units. There will be five.

5. Sew the final seam in each unit, finger pressing the center seams in opposite directions to avoid bulk on one side. Press.

Constructing Unit B

1. Place a #2 dark triangle on top of a #3 light triangle, right sides of the fabrics together. Place a pin through the dot on the dark triangle, poking down into the dot on the light triangle. This method will keep the pieces straight, since the points of the two triangles do not line up perfectly for sewing. Place a pin through the dots at the opposite end of the triangles also.

2. Stitch the two triangles together. Press the seam in the direction of the dark triangle.

3. Sew another dark triangle to the opposite side of the light triangle, using the same method of matching the dots to pin the ends. Press. This completes one Unit B. Repeat to make three more.

Sewing the Units Together

The units will now be sewn together to form rows. There are three rows in this block.

1. Stitch the units in Row 1 together and then press the seams in one direction.

2. Stitch the units in Row 2 together and press the seams in the direction opposite from that in Row 1.

3. Stitch the units in Row 3 together and press the seams in the same direction as in Row 1.

4. Sew Row 1 to Row 2, placing straight pins at the intersections of the seams (which have been finger pressed in opposite directions to eliminate excess bulk). Pins are placed perpendicular to the edge and far enough away from the edge so that they will not be in the way of the needle.

5. Sew Row 3 onto the above section, using the same method.

6. Your block is now complete. It should measure 12½″ square. Give it a final pressing on the right side, making sure the seams between the rows are pressed in one direction.

HAND PIECING: PRECISION IS THE NAME OF THE GAME

Hand piecing gives a soft edge to the seams and, with small, even running stitches in rhythmic motion, allows the quilter who enjoys hand work to produce beautiful hand-pieced quilts. This method gives more accuracy and control than machine piecing, allowing you to make precise curved seams (see the *Drunkard's Path* quilt on page 86 and the practice exercise below) and some of the more complex pieced patterns. Because you never stitch into the seam allowance, you can turn any seam allowance in any direction; you therefore have more freedom in the sew order.

MAKING TEMPLATES FOR HAND PIECING

Templates for hand piecing are made in exactly the same way as for machine sewing.

MARKING AND CUTTING THE FABRIC

1. With the wrong side facing up, place a single thickness of fabric on your cutting board.
2. Arrange the templates on the fabric, the grainline on the templates corresponding to the lengthwise grain of the fabric.
3. Using a sharp lead, white, gray or silver pencil, trace around each template.
4. Fold the fabric up to four thicknesses with the marked portion on top. Secure with pins inside the marked lines to hold the layers in place. Cut the fabric pieces apart using your fabric scissors, taking long, even strokes, or use the rotary cutter, wide plastic ruler and cutting board to cut on all the marked lines.
5. Use the small C-Thru ruler and pencil to mark the stitching line on the wrong side of every fabric piece. The stitching line is 1/4" in from the cutting line.

After the fabric pieces have been cut and marked, organize them according to the sew order required by the pattern. It is helpful to store them in a flat box with a picture of your pattern on the front, along with a diagram of the sew order. You can also then organize into smaller portable containers those you wish to take along to seam while you have some free time.

Wrong side of fabric

Step 5

SEWING THE PIECES

In hand piecing, the running stitch is the preferred stitch for sewing the fabric pieces together. You will want three to five stitches on your needle at one time.

1. To thread your needle (#10 Between), cut approximately 18" of cotton thread diagonally—the resulting sharper end will enter the eye easily. Use a single strand of thread without a knot. ✳ *Helpful hint:* The eye of the Between needle is small and can be difficult to thread. A needle

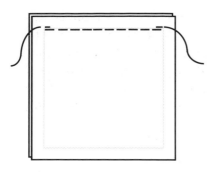

Step 3

SUPPLIES:
1/4 yd. each of two fabrics (one light, one dark)
Template plastic
Black ultra-fine permanent pen
Gray, white or silver pencil
Paper scissors
Fabric scissors
Glass-head pins
Sequin pins
Needle, #10 Between
Cotton thread
Small scissors
Drafting tape
Ultra-fine sandpaper
Small C-Thru ruler
Steam iron
Pressing surface
Light-colored towel

threader may be useful.

2. Place the two pieces of fabric to be sewn right sides together and use pins placed at right angles to the sewing line to secure. Place pins at the beginning and ending points to avoid any possible shifting.

3. Starting at the beginning of the marked line, take two small backstitches leaving a 1″ tail. Then continue across the line with small running stitches. Keep the tension even, neither too tight nor too loose. When you reach the end of the marked line take two backstitches. Cut the thread, leaving a 1″ tail. *Do not make knots.*

This hand piecing gives great control over fitting shapes together so they match perfectly at the junctions. *Never stitch into the seam allowances;* stitch only on the line. Then, when needed, flip back the seam allowance and continue sewing. Check often to see that the marked line on the front piece is lined up with the marked line of the back piece. Sew the pieces together in units, as we discussed earlier under machine piecing.

PRACTICE EXERCISE: Making a 12″ *Drunkard's Path* block

1. Lay your template plastic over template patterns 5e and 5g found on page 152 and secure with drafting tape.

2. Use the permanent pen and small C-Thru ruler to trace accurately around the outside of the two template patterns.

3. Remove the tape and plastic.

4. Use your paper scissors to cut out the two plastic templates carefully, just inside the marked lines.

5. Use your permanent pen to mark the following on each template:
    Block: *Drunkard's Path*
    Template #: 5e or 5g
    Block size: 12″
    Direction of lengthwise grain and center mark on curves

6. With the wrong side facing up, place a single thickness of fabric on top of the rough side of the sandpaper. Lay the plastic template on top of the fabric, making sure the lengthwise marking on the template corresponds to the lengthwise grain of the fabric. Using a pencil, mark around the template. Do not press so hard as to push the true size of the template

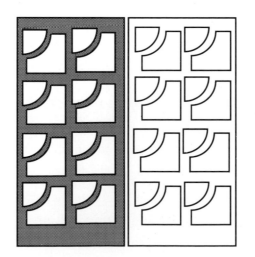

Step 6

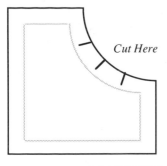

Cut Here

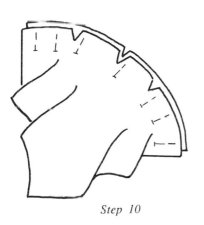

Cut Here

Steps 8-9

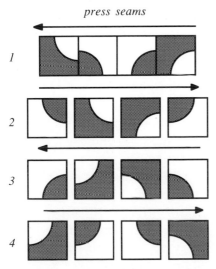

Step 10

press seams

Steps 12-13

pattern out of shape. If you are using *non-directional* fabric, you can cut up to four thicknesses simultaneously. Make sure the fabric has a smooth surface and the selvages are even. The folds need to be kept in place either with a light pressing or with a few pins. If you are using a *directional* printed fabric, you will not be able to see how the layers underneath are being cut, so you will want to cut a single thickness. Cut the following for your practice block:

- Light fabric—eight each of templates 5e and 5g.
- Dark fabric—eight each of templates 5e and 5g.

7. If you are cutting just one thickness of fabric, use sharp scissors and take long cutting strokes. If you are cutting multiple layers and using scissors, pin the fabrics together inside the outline of the template pattern to keep the layers united and prevent them from slipping.

8. Use your small C-Thru ruler to mark the stitching lines and the center of the curves on each fabric piece. Stitching lines are indicated with dotted lines on the template patterns.

9. Use the small scissors to make clips (stopping 1/16″ from the stitching line) at the center of the curves on all fabric pieces.

10. With right sides of the fabrics together, lay a concave curved piece on top of a convex curved piece of the opposite color, matching up the center clips. Place sequin pins at the clips to hold the pieces in place. Also line up the two pieces on the straight seam lines and place pins to hold them securely. Place two more pins along the curved edges to keep them even for stitching.

11. Use hand-piecing techniques to sew the units together.

12. Lay the units out *exactly* as shown in the diagram.

13. Sew the four units in Row 1 together and press their seams in one direction.

14. Sew the four units in Row 2 together and press their seams in the direction opposite from that in Row 1.

15. Repeat for Rows 3 and 4, alternating the direction of the seams.

16. Place Row 1 on top of Row 2 with the right sides together. Place pins at the seam intersection so the seams will remain turned in opposite directions. Sew the two rows together.

17. Attach Rows 3 and 4 in the same manner.

18. Press the seams between the rows on the wrong, then right, side.

19. The block is complete and should measure 12½″.

APPLIQUÉ: A PAPER-BASTING METHOD

Appliqué is as much a part of quiltmaking as is piecing. With it, designs are made by cutting pieces of one fabric and *applying* them to the surface of another. You can do much more than just take a single design and stitch it to a background fabric: you can create intricate designs by combining several elements. The paper-basted method of appliqué taught by Adele Ingraham allows you to make simple, elaborate or complex designs such as flowers, birds, animals, figures, hearts or symbols. You have the option of making stylized or realistic designs because of the precision in making stems, curves, points and V's. This method allows you to:

1. reproduce intricate shapes accurately from a line drawing;
2. duplicate shapes exactly;
3. place shapes flat on the background fabric;
4. handle very small shapes easily;
5. make smooth, even curves and sharp points and V's.

PREPARATION OF PATTERN

1. Trace or make a photocopy of the entire pattern.

2. Trace the required number of shapes for the overall design onto a piece of plain paper (5 circles or 12 leaves, for example). Leave spaces between the shapes for easier cutting. Do not trace any stems: they will be made from bias strips of fabric. ✻ *Helpful hint:* Use a plastic circle template to make accurate circles. Mark the grainline on each shape.

3. Use your paper scissors to cut out all of the individual shapes. Since the shape you cut will be the shape you get, take time to cut accurately. ✻ *Helpful hint:* If any shape in the pattern you have chosen (such as a leaf) has long, thin points, redraw the shape to have broader points. It will look just as good and will be easier to handle.

PREPARATION AND MARKING OF BACKGROUND FABRIC

1. Press the fabric you plan to use as a background.

2. Cut out the background fabric, keeping the grainline straight, allowing a 1/4″ seam allowance on all sides. (A 12″ finished block would be cut 12½″.)

3. Turn the background fabric to the wrong side and, with a lead pencil, write the word "Top" and indicate the direction of the lengthwise grain in the seam allowance at the top of the block.

4. With the right side of the background fabric facing up, center it on top of the overall traced or photocopied design. Hold it in place with drafting tape. Using a #2.5 lead pencil, lightly trace 1/16″ inside each shape. In addition, stems are marked with a single line through the middle. ✻ *Helpful hint:* When tracing a pattern onto fabric, tape the pattern to a daylight window and tape the piece of fabric over it. Then use a lead pencil to lightly trace around the pattern. Another option is to make your own light table. Use a glass table or place a piece of Plexiglas

over a dining table which has been opened for insertion of its extension leaves. Place a lamp underneath the glass or Plexiglas. Place the pattern on the glass or Plexiglas and the fabric over the pattern. Lightly trace onto the fabric. This method works especially well when tracing onto dark fabrics.

PREPARATION OF STEMS

Stems are made from bias strips of fabric. Here are two methods of construction.

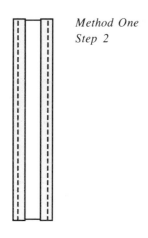

Method One
Step 2

METHOD ONE

1. Cut a bias strip of fabric 1/2" wide by 25" long. This can be made from 1/2 yard of fabric.

2. Fold both 25" edges 1/8" to the wrong side and hold them in place with a small basting stitch.

3. Lay the bias strip directly over the stem placement lines on the pattern, following the curves on the pattern. Cut the strip where appropriate. Pin the bias strips into place on the pattern.

4. Press all bias strips while they are still pinned to the pattern. This will pre-shape the strips and prevent them from puckering.

5. Remove the strips from the pattern.

METHOD TWO: Utilizing bias bars or 1/4" flat metal strips

1. Cut a bias strip of fabric 7/8" wide by 25" long. This can be made from 1/2 yard of fabric.

2. Fold the bias strip in half lengthwise with the right side facing out.

3. Machine stitch along the lengths with an accurate *1/8" seam allowance*. This will create a tube.

4. Insert the metal strip into the fabric tube and place the seam line in the center of a flat side of the bar.

5. With the metal strip still inserted in the fabric, steam press on both sides. The seam allowance is pressed to one side.

6. Remove the metal strip.

7. Complete Steps 3-5 in Method One above.

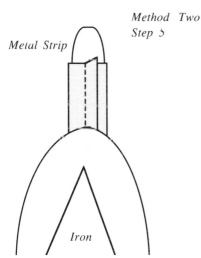

Method Two
Step 5

Metal Strip

Iron

PINNING AND BASTING PAPER PATTERNS TO FABRIC

1. With the grainline marking facing you, lay the individual paper patterns on the wrong side of the fabric, leaving at least 1/2" between shapes. The grainline marking on the paper pattern must correspond to the lengthwise grain of the fabric.

2. Pin the paper pattern in place with sequin pins.

3. Using small scissors, cut out the fabric around the shape, 1/4" larger than the paper pattern.

4. Baste the paper pattern to the fabric. Remove the pins.

5. This step involves basting the seam allowance down to the wrong side of the paper pattern. Preparation for basting varies from shape to shape. Specific instructions follow:

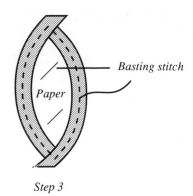

Basting stitch

Paper

Step 3

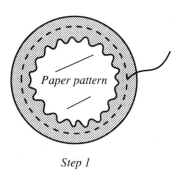

Paper pattern

Step 1

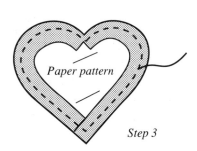

Paper pattern

Step 3

a. Leaves (and other shapes with points, such as hearts)
  (1) Thread your needle with a single strand of thread and place a knot in one end. With the paper pattern facing you, fold the seam allowance toward you.
  (2) Starting on a curved side of the shape (and not at its point), bring the needle up from the right side (so that the knot is on the right side). Take small running stitches to hold the seam allowance in place.
  (3) Stitch right up to the point, then fold the seam allowance from the opposite side of the shape beyond the point and continue stitching. When you look at the right side of the shape, there should be an excess piece of fabric extending out beyond the point. This will be tucked under when the shape is sewn to the background fabric. *Do not cut it off.*
  (4) Press on the wrong, then right, side.

b. Circles
  (1) Thread your needle with a single strand of thread and place a knot in one end. With the paper pattern facing you, take small running stiches 1/8″ away from the edge of the paper pattern, drawing up the thread as you sew. This will distribute the fullness evenly. Continue all the way around the circle. This row of stitching will not be removed.
  (2) Baste again around the edge of the circle through all layers to hold the seam allowance flat.
  (3) Press on the wrong, then right, side.

c. Scallops (and shapes with V's, such as hearts)
  (1) At each V make a small, straight clip into the seam allowance, stopping 1/16″ from the edge of the paper pattern.
  (2) With the paper side up, fold the seam allowance toward you. Thread your needle with a single strand of thread and place a knot in one end. Bring the needle up from the right side (so that the knot is on the right side). Folding the clipped edges of the V's out sideways to form an inverted V, take small running stitches to hold the seam allowance in place.
  (3) Continue around the shape. Cut the thread at the end, leaving a 1″ tail.
  (4) Press on the wrong, then right, side.

PLACEMENT OF PAPER-BASTED PIECES TO A BACKGROUND FABRIC

1. Shapes which appear closest to the background fabric, or which will have other shapes extending over part of them, are positioned first. This generally applies to stems. Position the pre-shaped stems one at a time over the marked lines on the background fabric. Pin and then baste them in place.

2. Stitch them to the background fabric with a back whipstitch along both sides.

3. Leaves are placed on next. One at a time, pin, then baste, the leaves into position on the background fabric.

4. Starting on a curved side of the leaf, not at its point, stitch it in place using the back whipstitch. Stitch right up to the point. At the point, use the tip of your needle or your small scissors to tuck the excess fabric under the point. Take one extra, tiny stitch to hold it in place. Stitch around the opposite side, repeating the procedure at the other point and continuing around the curve, stopping 1/2" from the starting point.

5. Remove the basting threads.

6. Use your tweezers to reach into the opening and remove the paper pattern.

7. Sew up the opening. End the stitching with two small backstitches on the wrong side.

8. Some small shapes are combined with larger shapes to form one unit before applying them to the background fabric, for example, centers to flowers or small flower buds to leaves. Place the smaller shape onto the larger shape, having their grainlines parallel. Hand stitch the small shape in place using a back whipstitch, stopping in time to remove the paper pattern.

9. Flowers with or without centers are placed on next. Pin, and then baste, the flowers in place.

10. Stitch the flowers to the background fabric using a back whipstitch, stitching all the way around the shape. End with two small backstitches on the wrong side. Remove the basting threads.

11. Turn the design to the wrong side. Cut out the background fabric underneath the flower to within 1/4" of the stitching line. This is done on any large shape to eliminate any excess bulk and prevent one color from shadowing through to another.

12. Finally, place the block, wrong side up, on a light-colored towel. Press firmly. Turn the block right side up and press lightly.

SUPPLIES:
**1/2 yd. of light fabric for back-
  ground**
1/2 yd. of green fabric for stems
1/4 yd. of green print for leaves
**1/8 yd. of yellow fabric for flower
  centers**
1/4 yd. of red fabric for flowers
Plain paper
#2.5 lead pencil
Thread
Needle, #10 Between
Sequin pins
Small scissors
Paper scissors
Drafting tape
Steam iron
Pressing surface
Light-colored towel
Tweezers
Sewing machine (optional)
Plastic circle template (optional)
**Bias bar *or* flat metal strip, 1/4″
  wide (optional)**

Practice Exercise: Making a 12″ *Benicia Rose* block

1. Make a photocopy or trace the entire design onto a piece of paper. The design can be found on page 156. The block is shown in color, framed on the wall in the Christmas shot, on page 7.

2. Using this paper, trace all shapes needed onto another piece of plain paper and cut them out, using paper scissors. Mark the lengthwise grain line on each paper piece. Complete "Preparation of Pattern" in the general instructions above.

3. Cut a 12½″ square of background fabric, marking "Top" and grain-line. Mark the placement of the shapes onto the right side of the back-ground fabric. Complete "Preparation and Marking of Background Fabric" in the general instructions.

4. Make the stems using either Method One or Method Two described in "Preparation of Stems" in the general instructions.

5. Pin and baste the individual paper shapes to the appropriate fabric. See "Pinning and Basting Paper Patterns to Fabric" in the general in-structions.

6. Pin, baste and then sew the individual shapes to the background fabric in the following sequence, removing the paper pattern after each application: stems, leaves, flowers. Refer to "Placement of Paper-Basted Pieces to a Background Fabric."

7. Press the completed block firmly on its wrong side, then lightly on its right.

CHAPTER 6

SEWING BLOCKS TOGETHER

SUPPLIES:
Reducing glass
Sewing machine *or* **hand-sewing**
 needle
Thread
Glass-head pins
Plastic right-angle triangle
Plain paper
Steam iron
Pressing surface
Light-colored towel
Lead pencil
Wide plastic ruler
Cutting board
Rotary cutter
Plastic or metal tape measure
Design board (optional)

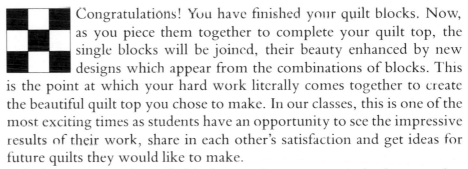Congratulations! You have finished your quilt blocks. Now, as you piece them together to complete your quilt top, the single blocks will be joined, their beauty enhanced by new designs which appear from the combinations of blocks. This is the point at which your hard work literally comes together to create the beautiful quilt top you chose to make. In our classes, this is one of the most exciting times as students have an opportunity to see the impressive results of their work, share in each other's satisfaction and get ideas for future quilts they would like to make.

Before you sew the quilt blocks together, you must check to see that the blocks are "squared-up" (all the same size). If you are making 12″ blocks, they should all measure 12½″. If there are any that are too big, just trim them a little. If one is a little too small, place a pin in it to remind yourself to compensate for its size when you set the blocks together. Read through the descriptions of the different types of sets below and experiment with your blocks to see which setting you like best.

If you are making a *Sampler* quilt, you will want to organize your blocks by color to achieve a pleasing result. ✳ *Helpful hint:* To do this, put the blocks up on a wall that has been covered with a piece of polyester felted fleece or a piece of white flannel (this design board allows the blocks to stick, and you can easily move them around). Visually, you see things better if they are vertical. You will be able to make better judgments. First pick up the blocks, not arranging them in any particular order, and place them on the wall. Next, take your reducing glass, step back six feet or so and look at the arrangement. Choose the blocks that jump out at you, the ones that attract your attention. These blocks usually fall into one or more of the following categories: very dark, dark and light contrast, bright and bold, yellow and red. Place these blocks in the center of the quilt or in the four corners. Use the remainder of the blocks to fill in the spaces, balancing color and design. (See the scrap *Sampler* quilt on the nursery wall on page 9).

STRAIGHT SETS

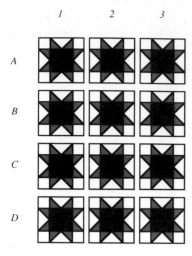

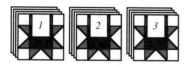

Step 1

Step 2

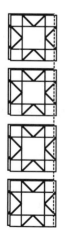

Steps 3-5

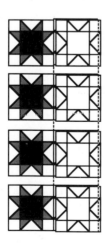

Step 6

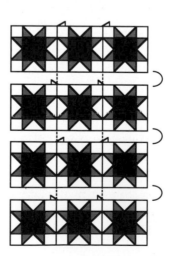

Steps 9-10

In a straight set, the quilt blocks are sewn together in vertical and horizontal rows.

1. Lay out all the quilt blocks on the floor or on your design board in the desired arrangement. Look at the entire set (all of your blocks) through the reducing glass. This will help you correct any errors. When you are satisfied with the arrangement, pin pieces of paper, marked #1, #2, #3, etc., on the first block in each vertical row. Horizontal rows are indicated with letters. ✱ *Helpful hint:* At this time, if any block is significantly too small, add an inch-wide frame of your background fabric, then trim the block to the needed size.

2. Pick up Block 1A and place it on top of Block 1B; then place these two on top of Block 1C, then 1D, etc. When you have completed this stack, repeat for Rows 2, 3, etc.

3. Take the stack of blocks in Row 1 and Row 2 to the sewing machine. Place Block 2A on top of 1A, right sides together. Stitch them together on the right-hand edge.

4. Without breaking the thread, place Block 2B on top of 1B and feed them through the machine right behind the previous pair.

5. Repeat this procedure for the remainder of the blocks in Rows 1 and 2. *Do not cut the threads holding the blocks together.*

6. Pick up the stack of Row 3 blocks. With the right sides together, place Block 3A on top of Block 2A and stitch them together along the right-hand edge. Repeat for the remainder of the blocks in Row 3, continuing to chain them through the machine.

7. Add the stack of Row 4 blocks, then Row 5 blocks, etc., until all the blocks have been sewn together.

8. Press the new seams in Row A in one direction; press the new seams in Row B in the opposite direction. Continue pressing Rows C, D, etc., alternating the pressed direction of the seams.

9. Fold Row A face down on top of Row B. Pin them together at the intersections of their seams. Ease or stretch the blocks to fit, if necessary. The seams were pressed in opposite directions so they will lock in place. Stitch these rows together, being careful to check that the seam lines of the blocks match up.

10. Fold Row B face down on top of Row C and repeat the procedure. Repeat for the remaining rows.

11. The quilt blocks are now all sewn together and form a quilt top. Give them a final pressing, then proceed to Chapter 7.

DIAGONAL SETS

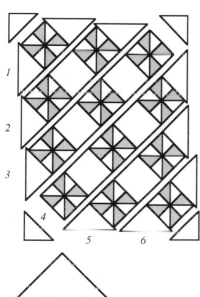

When the quilt blocks are turned on point and sewn together, this is called a diagonal set. All the blocks must be laid out on the floor or on a design board, so you can view them through the reducing glass to see the complete design before sewing and thereby avoid mistakes.

You will note that side triangles are necessary to square up the quilt around the edges. The fabric used for these triangles can be one already used in the blocks or something entirely different which will give the feeling that the blocks are suspended in space.

MAKING SIDE TRIANGLES

1. When all the quilt blocks are laid out on the floor, count to see how many side triangles are necessary (do not include corners).

Total number of triangles = (a) _____

Divide this number by 4 = (b) _____. Round up to the nearest whole number. This gives the number of squares of fabric to cut.

Next, take the diagonal measurement of a block = (c) _____

Add _____2"_____

Total = (d) _____

2. Cut the number of squares of fabric written on line (b) to the measurement written on line (d).

3. Cut the squares into quarters diagonally.

4. Lay these triangles around the edges of the quilt.

MAKING THE CORNER TRIANGLES

1. Cut two squares of fabric the size of your block plus 1½″ (i.e., if your blocks measure 12″, cut two 13½″ squares). Cut these in half diagonally.

2. Lay these triangles out on the floor in the corners of the quilt.

NOTE: Making the triangles in this manner will result in a straight grain of fabric running around the entire edge of the quilt. This is important, as there will be less stretch than if triangles were cut on the bias, as

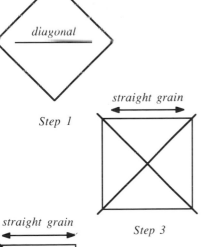

diagonal

Step 1

straight grain

Step 3

straight grain

Step 1

is sometimes done. ✷ *Helpful hint:* These triangles will all be a little too big, but the excess will be cut away when a border or binding is attached. This method, developed by Mary Ellen Hopkins, is easier than trying to determine the exact size of the triangle and then piecing it into the side of the quilt.

ASSEMBLING THE QUILT TOP

1. With a piece of paper, mark diagonal Rows 1, 2, 3, 4, etc. These rows *will include the side triangles*.

2. Stitch the blocks in Row 1 together, then Row 2, etc.

3. Press the new seams in Row 1 in one direction. Press the new seams in Row 2 in the opposite direction. Repeat for the remaining rows, alternating the direction of the new seams.

4. Placing pins at the seam intersections, stitch Row 1 to Row 2. Then add Row 3, then Row 4, etc.

5. Sew on the four corner triangles.

6. Since your side triangles are too large, the sides of the quilt top need to be trimmed and straightened before you add borders. Take the quilt top to the cutting board and use the wide plastic ruler and rotary cutter to straighten up the edges of the quilt and remove the excess fabric. ✷ *Helpful hint:* Check to see that opposite sides are the same measurement and that the corners are at right angles.

7. Give the quilt top a final pressing before proceeding to Chapter 7.

DESIGN OPTIONS

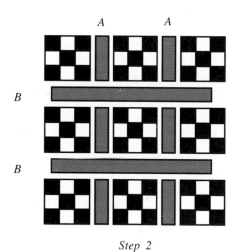

Step 2

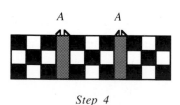

Step 4

ALTERNATE BLOCKS

One quick and easy way of enlarging your quilt and reducing the total number of pieced or appliquéd blocks is with the use of alternate blocks. The easiest alternate blocks are plain blocks which are set between the pieced or appliquéd blocks. They can be used in either a straight or a diagonal setting. See the *Bear's Paw* quilt on page 64, *Pine Tree* quilt on page 61 and the *Basket* quilt on page 81 as examples of quilts with alternate blocks.

SASHING

Strips of fabric separate and frame the individual blocks. See the planned *Sampler* quilt on page 9.

To use sashing in your quilt:

1. Lay all the quilt blocks on the floor or design board in the desired arrangement.

2. Determine the required number of A and B strips necessary.

3. Cut all the A strips the desired finish width plus *1/2" seam allowance*. The length of these strips will be the same measurement as the blocks.

4. Sew the A strips between the blocks in Row 1. Repeat for the remaining rows. Press the seams in the direction of the A strips.

5. Measure across Row 1. Using this measurement, cut the required number of B strips.

6. Lay a B strip on top of the bottom edge of Row 1, right sides together. Sew.

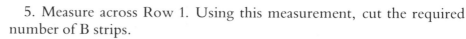

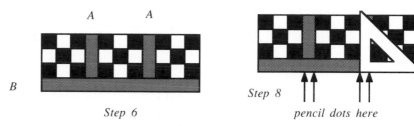

Step 6

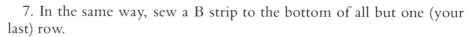

Step 8   *pencil dots here*

7. In the same way, sew a B strip to the bottom of all but one (your last) row.

8. With your right-angle triangle, place pencil dots on the B strips as indicated in the diagram.

9. Pin Row 2 to the B strip of Row 1, being *very careful* to match the pencil dots *exactly*. Ease in any fullness if necessary while sewing in order to keep the strips straight.

10. Continue the same process with the remainder of the rows.

11. Give the completed quilt top a final press.

NOTE: When sashing is used in a diagonal setting, add the width of the sashing to the diagonal measurement when determining the size of the side and corner triangles.

Steps 9-10

POSTS

Pieces of fabric join sashing to sashing at the intersection of the blocks. See the *Heart* quilt on page 70.

To use posts in your quilt:

1. Lay all the blocks on the floor or your design board to determine the total number of sashing strips and posts that are needed.

2. Complete Steps 3 and 4 in the sashing instructions above.

3. Use the width measurement of the sashing strips to cut squares of fabric for the required number of posts.

4. Cut the B sashing strips the desired finished width plus *1/2" seam allowance.*

5. For each row, sew the B strips to the posts, as shown in the diagram. Press the seams in the direction of the B strips.

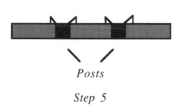

Posts

Step 5

6. Lay one of these finished B strips on top of the bottom of Row 1, right sides together. Align the posts in your B strip with the A strips and secure with pins. Sew.

7. In the same way, sew a B strip to the bottom of all but one (your last) row.

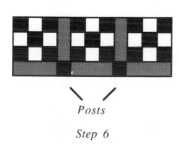

Posts

Step 6

8. Pin Row 2 to the B strip of Row 1, being *very careful* to match all posts with their A strips. Ease in any fullness if necessary while sewing in order to keep the strips straight.

9. Continue the same process for the remainder of the rows.

10. Give the quilt top a final press.

CHAPTER 7

ADDING BORDERS

SUPPLIES:
Reducing glass
Sewing machine *or* hand-sewing
    needle
Thread
Glass-head pins
Plastic right–angle triangle
Steam iron
Pressing surface
Light-colored towel
Wide plastic ruler
Cutting board
Rotary cutter or scissors
Plastic or metal tape measure
Design board (optional)

 Borders affect the total design of the quilt. Often, even experienced quiltmakers give too little attention to the question of borders and to the selection of border designs and fabric. A simple geometric pattern can be enhanced by a border. Likewise, a complex, well-crafted quilt top can lose much of its appeal if the border is not carefully selected.

A border can appear as a separate frame for the quilt top, it can repeat colors, fabrics or patterns from the quilt top, wholly or in part, or it may combine several of these traits. When you have completed your quilt top, pin it up on a design board and look at it through your reducing glass. This allows you to experiment with borders and see their relationship in size and pattern to the quilt top.

There are many different types of borders from which to choose. Look through the quilts in Chapter 2 for ideas or design your own, remembering:

• A border can enhance a rather simple pattern to make it more interesting. See the *Fence Rail* quilt on page 29.

• Repeating a color or fabric design used in the quilt top can help to unify your quilt. See the *Thousand Pyramids* quilt on page 69.

• Wide borders of an unrelated fabric will give added interest and texture. See the *Wild Goose Chase* variation on page 43.

• Some patterns are complete in design without a border (see the *Log Cabin* quilt on page 30) and, sometimes, a border is a distraction, not an asset.

• A border can be a single strip of fabric (see Pat Callis's *Wild Goose Chase* quilt on page 40) or multiple strips of fabric (see the *Pine Tree* quilt on page 61). There are no set rules as to the number and width of borders.

• Borders can be pieced, as in the sawtooth border around the *Bear's Paw* quilt on page 64: it is made simply from half-square triangles. The border on the *Madison House* quilt is another option (see page 52).

Your borders can be either straight or mitered. The difference between the two lies in the treatment of the corners. Either method is acceptable; it is simply a matter of preference. Often the type of border you choose will dictate the method of attachment. For example, you would generally not miter a pieced border.

DETERMINING YARDAGE FOR BORDERS

Yardage is based on 44″-wide fabric.

DETERMINING YARDAGE FOR STRAIGHT BORDERS

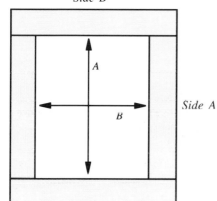

Side B

Side A

CUTTING (All measurements in inches)

Side A:

1. Dimension A, through center of quilt		_____ ″
2. Working allowance: add 4″	+	4″
3. For sides A, you will need 2 strips, each	=	_____ ″

Side B:

4. Dimension B, through center of quilt	_____ ″	
5. Width of border × 2	+ _____ ″	
6. Total (Steps 4 + 5)		_____ ″
7. Working allowance: add 4″	+	4″
8. For sides B, you will need 2 strips, each	=	_____ ″

YARDAGE

Border width:	Total yards required:
0″ – 11″	Larger of Step 3 or Step 8 ÷ 36″ = _____ yds
11⅛″ – 22″	Steps 3 + 8 ÷ 36″ = _____ yds.

DETERMINING YARDAGE FOR MITERED BORDERS

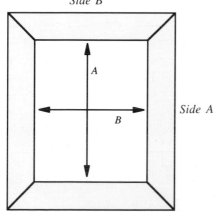

Side B

Side A

CUTTING (All measurements in inches)

Side A:

1. Dimension A, through center of quilt		_____ ″
2. Width of border × 2	+	_____ ″
3. Total (Steps 1 + 2)		_____ ″
4. Working allowance: add 9″	+	9″
5. For sides A, you will need 2 strips, each	=	_____ ″

Side B:

6. Dimension B, through center of quilt _____ ″

7. Width of border × 2 + _____ ″

8. Total (Steps 6 + 7) _____ ″

9. Working allowance: add 9″ + _____9″

10. For sides B, you will need 2 strips, each = _____ ″

YARDAGE

Border width:	Total yards required:
0″ – 11″	Step 5 ÷ 36″ = _____ yds.
11⅛″ – 22″	Steps 5 + 10 ÷ 36″ = _____ yds.

CUTTING BORDERS

1. It is best to cut the borders on the lengthwise grain of the fabric, as there is less stretch. Therefore, using your cutting tools, remove one selvage edge from the fabric. Since you are working with a lot of fabric for the border, you may not be able to fit the entire length on the board. Cut as much as possible and then move the fabric to cut the rest.

2. Place your wide plastic ruler on top of the fabric to measure, and cut four strips the desired border width plus 1/2″ for seam allowances, adjusting the ruler along the length as you cut. If you are using a directional fabric or a border-printed fabric, take care to cut straight along the printed pattern.

3. Repeat for any additional borders.

ATTACHING STRAIGHT BORDERS

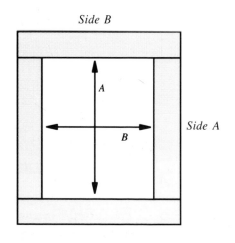

1. Lay the quilt top out on a flat surface and use the plastic or metal tape measure to determine dimensions A (the longer dimension) and B (the shorter dimension) across the center. Write these figures down.

2. You will be fitting the quilt top to the border strips *rather than* the border strips to the quilt top. This will prevent the edges of the borders from rippling. To achieve the best results, place pins at the center points of two border strips. Measure out from the pins in each direction a distance equal to one-half the A dimension. Place pins at these points to mark the corners.

3. Place pins at the center points along sides A of the quilt top.

4. Lay these border strips on each A side of the quilt top, right sides together, matching pins with corners and at the center points. Use more pins to hold the borders in place. Sew with the border strips on top, as

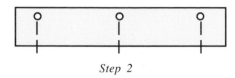

Step 2

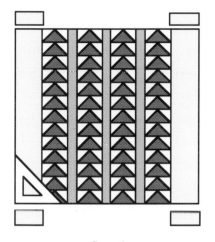

Step 6

they are more stable than the pieced quilt top and less likely to stretch. Ease in any fullness if necessary.

5. Press the fabrics flat to set the stitches in place. Fold the border strips back, over the stitching lines. Press them.

6. Use your cutting tools to trim the excess length of border fabric even with the B sides of the quilt top. Use your right-angle triangle to be certain that the corners are square.

7. Mark the two remaining border strips and the B sides of the quilt top, with pins at their center points. Measure out from the pins in each direction on the border strips, a distance equal to one-half the B dimension. Place pins at these points to mark the corners.

8. Attach these border strips to the quilt top using the same method described in Steps 4 and 5 above.

9. Use your cutting tools to trim the excess length of border fabric even with the A sides of the quilt top. Use your right-angle triangle to be certain that the corners are square.

10. Press on the right side.

Additional borders can be added if desired, using the same technique. *Always complete one border before adding another.*

Your quilt top is now ready to be marked and layered for quilting or tying.

ATTACHING CORNER BLOCKS

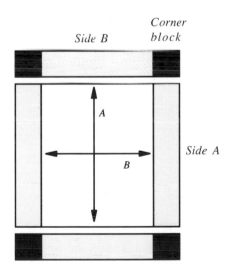

Step 4

A design option in planning borders is to add a corner block. This can solve a lot of problems if you are finding it difficult to turn the corner with pieced borders or if you do not have enough length of material to miter the corners. A corner block can often be the missing design element that adds that needed sparkle to your overall design. See the *Pine Tree* quilt on page 61.

1. Do Steps 1-6 in "Attaching Straight Borders" above.

2. Cut the two B border strips using the B dimension determined in Step 1 of that section.

3. Use the width measurement of the B border strips to cut squares of fabric for the corner blocks.

4. Sew a corner block to each end of the B border strips.

5. Place pins at the center points of sides B of the quilt top and the B border strips.

6. Refer to Steps 4 and 5 of "Attaching Straight Borders," matching up the seams at the corner blocks with the seams of the A border strips.

ATTACHING MITERED BORDERS

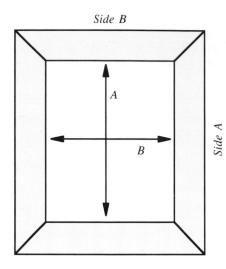

Side B

Side A

A

B

When more than one border is desired, match the center points of the borders to each other. Sew together lengthwise in one unit before sewing to the quilt top. Treat this unit now as one border strip and use the technique described below.

1. Using your plastic or metal tape measure, determine dimensions A and B of the quilt top across its center. Write these figures down.

2. You will be fitting the quilt top to the border strips *rather than* the border strips to the quilt top. This will prevent the edges of the borders from rippling. To achieve the best results, place pins at the center points of two border strips. Measure out from the pins in each direction a distance equal to one-half the A dimension. Place pins at these points to mark the corners.

3. Place pins at the center points along sides A of the quilt top.

4. Lay these border strips on each A side of the quilt top, right sides together, matching pins with corners and at the center points. Use more pins to attach the borders in place. Beginning and ending *1/4" from each corner*, stitch the A borders to the quilt top, with the border strip on top, as it is more stable than the pieced quilt top and less likely to stretch. There will be a generous amount of fabric from both ends of the borders extending beyond the quilt top. This is needed to miter the corners. *Do not cut it off.*

5. Mark the center points on the two remaining border strips. Measure out from the pins, in each direction, a distance equal to one-half the B dimension. Place pins at these points to mark the corners.

6. Place pins at the center points along sides B of the quilt top.

7. Using the method described in Step 4, sew the B borders to the B sides of the quilt top.

8. Take the quilt top to your pressing surface. Working on one corner of the quilt at a time, extend the unsewn border ends out straight, overlapping the end of A over the end of B.

9. Lift up the A border strip and fold it under *only itself*, at a 45-degree angle. The remainder of border A should lie even with both sides of the underlying B border.

10. Using your right-angle triangle or ruler with a 45-degree angle, check to see that the angle is accurate and the corner is square. Place pins to hold the border strips in place. Then press to set the angle.

11. Turn the quilt to the wrong side and place pins near the pressed fold in the corner to hold the border strips in place.

12. Take the quilt top to the sewing machine and, wrong side up, stitch along the folded line in the corner. Be careful to stitch right up to the previous stitching lines in the corner of the quilt top to avoid gaps.

13. Trim all excess fabric from the border strips.

14. Press on the right side.

15. Repeat for the remaining three corners.

Your quilt top is now ready to be marked and layered for quilting or tying.

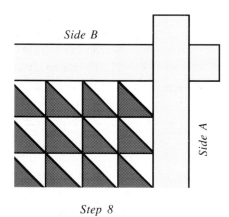

Side B

Side A

Step 8

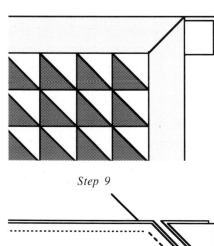

Step 9

Steps 12-13

ATTACHING BORDERS OF BORDER-PRINTED FABRIC

Border-printed fabrics are a quick and simple way of adding a new dimension to your quilt. It is important that the corners be the same, or at least that opposite corners match. Be sure to purchase extra fabric for matching. After the eye looks to the center of the quilt, it will be drawn out to the corners. These borders look best when the corners are mitered. If you are working on a square quilt, you will not have any difficulty in getting the designs to match in the corners, as long as you place a similar design at the center point of each side. A rectangular quilt is a little more challenging.

1. Use a metal or plastic tape measure to determine the A and B dimensions of the quilt top across the center. Write these figures down.

2. Place pins at the center points of each side of the quilt top.

3. You will be fitting the quilt top to the border strips *rather than* the border strips to the quilt top. This will prevent the edges of the borders from rippling. Choose a design in your border-printed fabric to be positioned at the center points of sides A of your quilt top. Mark it with pins. Measure out from the pins in each direction a distance equal to one-half the A dimension. Place pins at these points to mark the corners. Do the same on the other A border strip.

4. Lay these border strips on each A side of the quilt top, right sides together, matching pins with corners and at the center points. Use more pins to attach the borders in place. Beginning and ending 1/4″ from each corner, stitch the A borders to the quilt, with the border strips on top, as they are more stable than the pressed quilt top and less likely to stretch. There will be a generous amount of fabric from both ends of the borders extending beyond the quilt top. This is needed to miter the corners. *Do not cut it off.*

5. Take the quilt top to the pressing surface and fold all four unsewn extensions of the borders back to form 45-degree angles. Check the accuracy of the angles with a ruler marked with a 45-degree angle. Press a fold in the angles.

6. Take the quilt top to a flat surface. Lay a B border strip along the B side of the quilt top. Line up the same design in the border fabric chosen in Step 3 above with the center point of side B. The excess B border strip lengths must extend *under* the folded corners of the previously attached A border strips.

7. Pull the B border strip together at its center, forming a pleat. Watch the designs forming in the corners and continue pulling until you find one you like. Make sure you are pulling equal amounts from each end so that the corner designs will match each other. Now fold the pleat to the wrong side of the border strip and pin.

8. Repeat for the other B side of the quilt top.

9. Place pins in the corners to hold the joining of the A and B borders in place.

10. Turn each B border strip right side down on the quilt top. Place

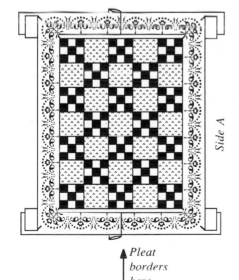

Side B

Side A

Pleat borders here

Steps 7-8

pins along the edge to attach it to the quilt top, pinning from the corners to the center pleat.

11. Fold the quilt top in half lengthwise, right side out. The pleats will extend beyond the center folds in the quilt top.

12. Stitch along each pleat even with the fold in the quilt top. Trim the excess to within 1/4″ of the stitching line. Press the seams in each B border strip to one side.

13. Unfold the quilt top and stitch your B border strips to it, beginning and ending 1/4″ from each corner.

14. To miter the corners, stitch along the folds which were pressed into the A border strips. For more details see Steps 11–13 in "Attaching Mitered Borders."

15. Press on the right side.

Your quilt top is now ready to be marked and layered for quilting or tying.

PIECED BORDERS

Borders constructed from the repetition of a single shape or a combination of shapes are called pieced borders. The shapes often repeat some that have been used in the quilt top. The most difficult task in designing a pieced border is deciding how to turn the corners. The design must flow smoothly and the corners must be the same or, at least, opposite corners must be the same. Pieced borders, once constructed into strips, are attached using the same method described for straight borders. Specific instructions for the samples referred to below are given in Chapter 2.

• Look at the *Bear's Paw* quilt on page 64. It has traditional sawtooth borders which zigzag around the edge of the quilt, causing the eye to travel the outer edge. In order to make the corners the same, the direction of the triangles in the center of each side was changed. The *T Blocks* quilt on page 38 also uses a sawtooth border with a different corner treatment.

• A good example of repeating a shape used in the pattern block is the border of the *Dresden Plate* quilt on page 76. The petal shape is combined with an equilateral triangle, forming a new, straight design. Notice that the design changes to turn the corners smoothly, giving the effect of a fan.

• The *Star of Bethlehem* quilt on page 84 uses a small *Sawtooth Star* in its border. Although both are stars, they are constructed of different shapes.

• Sometimes you may want a border unrelated to the pattern. This causes the border to stand apart. Look at the *Madison House* quilt on page 52, covering the border with plain paper to hide it. Now, remove the paper and see how the border adds a feeling of fun and whimsy.

CHAPTER 8

PREPARING TO QUILT

Now that your quilt top is complete, you must give some thought to how you would like to finish the quilt. That is, how would you like to secure the three layers (top, batting and backing) of the quilt together? Your quilt can be hand-quilted, machine-quilted or tied. Read through the description of each technique below, keeping in mind the amount of time you want to devote to finishing your quilt and how it will ultimately be used.

Hand Quilting. Small running stitches hold the three layers together, either following lines or patterns which have been marked on the quilt top or following the outline of a pieced or appliquéd block, or both. Hand quilting gives strength, dimension, texture and design to a quilt. It requires quite a bit of time and takes practice to make small, even stitches, but the result will be an heirloom.

Machine Quilting. Machine stitches hold the three layers of the quilt together. As in hand quilting, the stitches will follow a design which has been marked on the quilt top, or the stitches can be sewn in the seams around a pieced block. With some practice on your machine, you can achieve beautiful results.

Tying. Small square knots are taken through all layers to hold them together. This is the quickest method of finishing. It can also provide surface design. Sometimes, ribbon bows are added for decoration.

CHOOSING AND PLANNING THE QUILTING DESIGN

If you have decided to either hand or machine quilt, you will need to choose a quilting design. Give as much attention to the selection of the design as you did to the construction of your quilt. Keep in mind that quilting shows up more on solid fabrics than on prints.

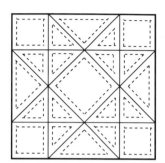

OUTLINE QUILTING

This follows the outline on either or both sides of a pieced or appliquéd block. Stitches can be made either very close to the seam line or 1/8″ to 1/4″ away. The outline quilting accentuates the shape. The shape around which you quilt will appear to come forward.

BACKGROUND QUILTING

This quilting fills large, often plain, spaces that you wish to make recede visually, allowing the more important patterns and designs to come forward. Our favorite background quilting lines are crossed diagonal lines because they are easy to make with a straight-edge ruler and simple to quilt.

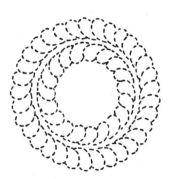

DESIGN QUILTING

These designs (such as wreaths, feathers, cables and baskets) work well in open spaces like alternate blocks, side and corner triangles and border areas. They are often combined with background quilting. See the *Star of Bethlehem* quilt on page 84.

There are many plastic quilting design templates available, including special ones for corners. Look for a design that appeals to you, relates well to the pattern of your quilt and fits nicely into the space you wish to quilt.

MARKING THE QUILTING DESIGNS ONTO THE QUILT TOP

Once you have selected your quilting designs, you will have to mark them onto your quilt top. This is done before the quilt is layered and basted. It can be a tedious job and takes a bit of planning and time. *Do not rush through this step.*

If you are planning to outline quilt, you can either stitch close to the seam line or stitch 1/8″ to 1/4″ away from it. If you are going to stitch close to the seam line, you will not have to mark the quilting line, although if you wish to quilt 1/4″ away from your seam line you can use a 1/4″ square Plexiglas rod to mark the quilting line.

If you have decided on a design for the border (such as a cable or feather), you will want the design to flow smoothly around the corner. Begin marking in the corners and work toward the center of the border.

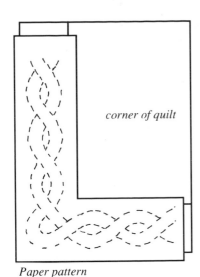

Paper pattern

✱ *Helpful hint:* Cut a strip of paper the exact size of the border, from the center point of one side to the center point of the other side (corner included). Trace the design onto the paper. You will be able to see where adjustments are needed before marking your fabric.

Keep a pencil sharpener close by. Use an artist's pencil (white, gray or silver) for marking the lines onto your quilt top. Test the marking pencil on a scrap of fabric before starting to mark on your quilt. Do *not* use water-soluble or disappearing marking pens: the ink may transfer into the batting and eventually re-appear on the quilt top.

Place a piece of ultra-fine sandpaper under the area of your quilt top to be marked. This prevents the fabric from slipping and the pencil from dragging. Marking as lightly as possible but visibly, mark the desired quilting line. Mark all the quilting lines on the entire quilt top.

BACKING FABRIC

As with the quilt top, it is important to choose a good-quality cotton fabric for your backing. Although a bed sheet may seem to be a good idea because of its convenient size, it is *not* suitable because the fabric is too tightly woven and you will have difficulty quilting through it.

When choosing the fabric for the backing, be sure to select a color that will not show through on the front, especially if the quilt top contains light colors; a dark, bright or bold print may show through. The backing can be a good opportunity to use a completely different fabric from those used on the top. Try something exciting for added interest. It is always fun to turn over a quilt and discover something unexpected.

Another option might be to piece the backing. It is a good way to use up some leftover lengths of fabric.

YARDAGE AND PREPARATION

Yardage is based on 44″-wide fabric.

1. Lay the quilt top on a flat surface and determine the A and B measurements.

2. You will want your cut backing fabric to be at least 2″ larger than the quilt top all the way around. Add 4″ for a "working allowance" to the A measurement. This is the measurement of one length.

3. Use this helpful chart to determine yardage for backing:

If dimension B is	# of lengths needed
0″–40″	1
41″–80″	2
81″–120″	3

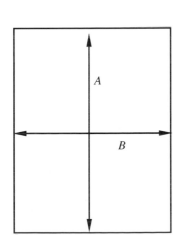

Step 1

4. If two or three lengths are required, cut the selvage edges off the lengths and stitch them together along the longer sides with a 1/4″ seam. Press the seam(s) to one side.

BATTING

Batting is the filling layer between the quilt top and the backing. Battings can be purchased in various weights, either pre-packaged and cut to a specified size or by the yard. There are also different types of batting. Look at the thickness before purchasing it. A thin batting will be easier to work with in hand quilting and give a more traditional look to your quilt, whereas a thicker batting is more suitable for machine quilting or tying and gives a down-like appearance. It is important to purchase a good-quality batting. The inexpensive battings may be too stiff and lose their resilience after washing. We advise that you purchase a batting which is soft, uniform in thickness and without lumps.

TYPES OF BATTING

100% Cotton or Cotton/Polyester Blends

A pure cotton batting with a low loft or a blend will give a traditional appearance to your finished quilt. It will require you to do very close quilting, with no more than 1/2″ between quilting lines, to achieve maximum durability in the quilt. Cotton batting has a tendency to shift and pull away if it is not quilted closely, causing it to lump. This batting can be used for either hand or machine quilting. An advantage to cotton batting is that it is non-allergenic and resists fiber migration. Fiber migration occurs when the tiny fibers of the batting surface creep through the quilt top, giving a lint-like appearance.

100% Polyester (Bonded)

The polyester battings can be purchased in various weights. The thicker batting will require less stitching but will be difficult for fine, even hand quilting. The low-loft or traditional polyester battings (less than 1/2″ thick) are suitable for hand quilting. The very heavy lofts and thick battings (more than 1/2″ thick) are used for tied quilts. But, remember—*polyester fibers migrate* more easily than do cotton fibers, and this problem is particularly noticeable on dark fabrics.

Before proceeding, check to see if:
1. The quilt top is pressed flat and without wrinkles.
2. All quilting lines are marked.
3. The backing is ready.
4. You have batting, either pre-cut or by the yard (buy the same number of lengths as you bought backing fabric).

If so, you are ready to proceed with layering your quilt and basting the layers together in preparation for quilting or tying. Follow the instructions for the technique you have chosen.

PREPARATION FOR QUILTING IN A HOOP

SUPPLIES:
Cotton thread
Glass-head pins
Batting
Masking tape
Cotton darning needle, #1
Paper scissors

1. Lay the backing fabric out on a smooth, flat surface, wrong side up. You can use a large table, a large cutting board or a floor. Do not use a good dining room table unless it is covered with a cloth and then a cutting board, because the needle will scratch the surface.

2. Pull the edges of the backing taut to eliminate any fullness or wrinkles, then tape it to your work surface. Tape the four center points first, then the four corners, keeping the edges as straight and the backing as square as possible.

3a. If you are using pre-cut batting, place the roll in the center of the backing fabric and gently unfold it, covering the backing. Smooth out any folds or creases. The batting now covers the entire backing fabric. –OR–

3b. If you are using batting purchased by the yard, you will need to butt the lengths together and, using a double strand of thread and a #1 cotton darning needle, sew them together with a diagonal basting stitch. Place the batting on top of the backing and smooth out any folds or creases.

4. Place the quilt top with the right side facing up on top of the batting, matching the center points of the quilt top to the center points marked on the backing fabric.

5. Pin through all layers with glass-head pins, starting in the center of the quilt and moving out to the edges. Place pins about 12″ apart. This will hold the layers together for hand basting.

6. With scissors, cut off the excess batting to within 1/2″ of all four of the quilt top sides.

7. Use a #1 cotton darning needle and cotton thread; cut a long length of thread (about 50″). Using a single thickness of thread without a knot in the end, start in the center of your quilt and work to the edge, making a long diagonal basting stitch to hold the layers together. Your stitches should form a 4″ grid.

8. Remove the masking tape and the pins. Fold the excess backing in half so that the raw edge of the backing comes up even with the raw edge of the quilt top. Fold the backing again, bringing the fold of backing over the edge of the quilt top 1/4″. Secure the folded edge of the backing to the quilt top with glass-head pins all the way around the edge of the quilt. With a running basting stitch, sew this folded edge through all three layers, removing the pins as you sew. This is an important step, because it will protect the edge of the quilt top from stretching and raveling and prevent the batting from linting out while you are quilting.

You are now ready to proceed to Chapter 9 and begin hand quilting.

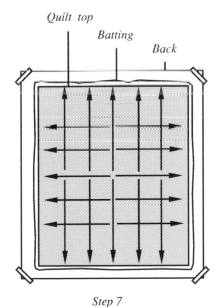

Quilt top
Batting
Back

Step 7

PREPARATION FOR QUILTING IN A FRAME

SUPPLIES:

Four "one-by-two" (really approximately 3/4″ × 1½″) boards (two should be 12″ longer than sides A of the backing; two should be 12″ longer than sides B. Purchase them at a lumber yard *and check to be sure that they are straight*.)
Four 2½″ C-clamps
Muslin (two pieces 5″ wide and as long as the A measurement of the backing and two pieces 5″ wide and as long as the B measurement)
Staple gun (*not* a hand stapler)
Cotton thread
Glass-head pins
Plastic right-angle triangle
Batting
Cotton darning needle, #1
Scissors

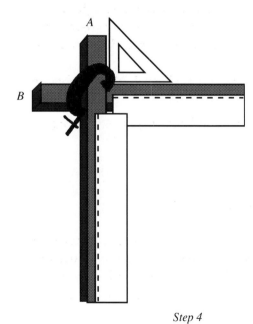

Step 4

MAKING AND USING YOUR OWN QUILT FRAME

1. Fold the pieces of muslin in half lengthwise with the raw edges even.

2. Mark the center point on one of the wider sides of each board and of each length of muslin.

3. Place the muslin pieces on top of the boards, center points matched, with the raw edge of the muslin centered on the board. Staple the muslin to the boards, placing staples at about two-inch intervals: these muslin pieces are now your four header strips.

4. This requires two people. ◘ *Warning:* Do not attempt to do it alone. Using your right-angle triangle, place an A board and a B board at right angles, stapled sides up, and secure them in place with a clamp at the corner. Repeat for the remaining three corners. The distance between the corners should be the same as the backing fabric for the quilt.

5. The frame must be elevated and supported. You can balance the boards on top of four straight-backed chairs.

6. Find the center points on the four header strips and mark them with glass-head pins. Also mark the center points on the four sides of the backing fabric.

7. With the wrong side of the backing fabric facing up, match the center points of the backing fabric to the center points of the header strips. Use pins to secure the backing to the header strips at these four points.

8. Using pins, secure the four corners of the backing to the header strips, measuring from the center points out to the corners to be sure that the distance is the same on each side.

9. Secure the rest of the backing to the header strips, easing in any fullness if necessary.

10a. If you are using pre-cut batting, place the batting in the center of the backing and gently unfold it to cover the backing. Smooth out any folds. –OR–

10b. If you are using batting purchased by the yard, you will need to butt the lengths together and, using a double strand of thread and a #1 cotton darning needle, sew them together with a diagonal basting stitch. Place the batting on top of the backing and smooth out any folds or creases.

11. Place pins at the center points on the four sides of the quilt top. Lay the quilt top on top of the batting, with the right side facing up, matching up the center points with those on the header strips. (The quilt top will be smaller than the batting and backing but the center points should line up.)

12. Measure from the center points to the corners of the quilt top, making sure the distances on opposite sides are the same, and pin the quilt top through the batting and backing all the way around the edges. ◘ *Warning:* This is an important step. Double-check to see that the

pinned quilt top is squared off and even; otherwise, your finished quilt will not be straight.

13. Make running basting stitches around the edge of the quilt through all three layers, removing the pins as you sew.

USING A READY-MADE FRAME

Follow the instructions which accompany your frame, using any of the above instructions and hints which will work to help you.

You are now ready to move on to Chapter 9 and begin hand quilting.

PREPARATION FOR MACHINE QUILTING

SUPPLIES:
Supplies listed for "Preparation for Quilting in a Hoop" *plus*
Steel safety pins, #1

1. Complete Steps 1-4 under "Preparation for Quilting in a Hoop" and prepare your quilt in the same manner.

2. Place #1 steel safety pins no more than 3″ apart throughout the entire quilt. Start pinning the center of the quilt and work out toward the edges. Be careful not to place the pins where you intend to machine stitch.

3. With scissors, cut off the excess batting to within 1/2″ of all four of the quilt top sides.

You are ready to move on to Chapter 9 and begin machine quilting.

PREPARATION FOR A TIED QUILT

SUPPLIES:
Supplies listed for "Preparation for Quilting in a Hoop"

A quilt can be tied either on a flat surface or in a frame. If you wish to use a flat surface such as a table or the floor, prepare the quilt as instructed in Steps 1-6 of "Preparation for Quilting in a Hoop." If you have a frame to use for tying, prepare the quilt as instructed in Steps 1-12 of "Preparation for Quilting in a Frame."

Proceed to Chapter 9 for instructions for tying your quilt.

CHAPTER 9

QUILTING

Many of our quilting students tell us that they find the time spent in quilting to be soothing. The relaxed, rhythmic motion of stitching is a calming contrast to our usual hectic, fast-paced lives. This leisurely activity allows quilters some quiet moments to get in touch with their feelings and thoughts.

Whereas many of the piecing techniques are quick, the hand quilting experience is not: even our most reluctant students admitted that they found the hand quilting experience to be very rewarding; they were pleased with their work and proud they had stuck with it. All the students were eager to share their work with fellow students, family members and friends. They found the praise they received for their hard work very gratifying.

Although three methods of completing your quilt are included below, we strongly recommend that at some point you devote some time to hand quilting. We feel that, in doing so, you will experience a new sense of yourself and share in the heartfelt tradition of hand quilting.

HAND QUILTING

SUPPLIES:
Quilting thread
Quilting hoop or frame
Needles, #9, #10 and #12 Betweens
Thimble
Small scissors
Needle grabber
Needle threader
Beeswax (optional)

If you will be quilting on a frame, you will begin quilting along the edges of the quilt and work in towards the center. If you will be quilting in a hoop, you will begin your quilting stitches in the center of the quilt and move to the edges. There are various sizes and shapes of hoops to choose from. ✷ *Helpful hint:* Purchase a size that feels comfortable to you, so that it is neither too small nor too large. We have had success working in a 14″ hoop. A good-quality wooden hoop is advised. Place the smaller ring of the hoop on a table. With the right side of the quilt facing up, position the area to be quilted on top of the smaller ring. Next, loosen the screw in the larger ring and lay it on top of the quilt, gently pushing it over the smaller ring. Smooth out any wrinkles in the quilt. Tighten up the screw in the larger ring to secure the quilt in place. The quilt should be neither too tight nor too loose in the hoop. You are ready to begin the quilting stitch.

THE QUILTING STITCH

There are two methods for beginning the quilting stitch, the Knot Method and the No-Knot Method. The Knot Method works well if you will be doing a lot of straight-line quilting without many starting and stopping points. The No-Knot Method works well on quilting designs such as wreaths, feathers or anything with several starting and stopping points.

The Knot Method
1. Cut a length of quilting thread approximately 24″ long.
2. Using a needle threader if necessary, thread your fine, short Between needle, and hold it with the point upwards.
3. To make a knot, hold the cut end of the thread between your index finger and the needle. Wrap the thread around the needle twice. Hold the thread in place with your fingers.
4. Without pulling so hard as to unthread the needle, carefully release the thread from between your fingers and slide the thread down and off the needle all the way to the other end of the thread. A knot should form at the end of the thread. This is a good method for making knots because it keeps them uniform in size.
5. Starting 1/2″ away from the line you wish to quilt on, stick the needle down through the quilt top and into the batting layer only. Do not go through to the backing. Bring the needle up on the line you wish to quilt on. Gently pull on the thread. The knot will be lying on the top of the quilt.
6. In order to hide the knot in the batting layer, gently tug on the thread with one hand and roll the thumbnail of the other hand over the top of the knot. This causes the knot to pop down into the batting layer.
7. Begin the quilting stitch with a very short backstitch.
8. Put on your thimble, take one small stitch with the thimble finger, going down all the way through the backing and up, working only on the tip of the needle. Place two fingers of the opposite hand underneath the quilt in order to feel the point of the needle as it goes down, and quickly push it to return it to the top. A quick return gives a small stitch. This should be done in a rocking motion—down-up-down-up-down-up—picking up about four stitches on the tip of the needle. Push the needle through. (Use your rubber thumb or piece of balloon at this point if it is difficult to bring the needle through.) ✳ *Helpful hint:* After you have pulled the thread taut, give just a little tug to move the position of the needle on the thread. This will prevent the thread from shredding at the eye of the needle. This is a very good habit to get into.
9. Repeat this step, picking up another four small stitches on the tip of

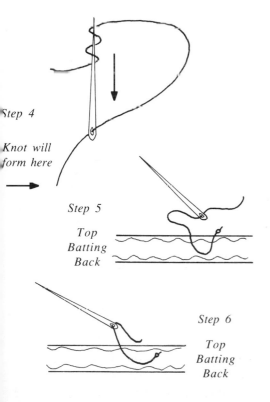

SUPPLIES:
Needles, #9, 10 or 12 Betweens
    There is no #11; the larger the number, the smaller the needle.
Quilting thread
    This thread has been waxed to slide more easily through all three quilt layers. If you are unable to find a color you like, you can use a regular spool of cotton or cotton/polyester thread provided you run it through beeswax before using it. Beeswax for this purpose can be purchased, with accompanying instructions.
Thimble
    Find one that fits comfortably on the middle finger of the hand you will be stitching with.
Small scissors
Grabber
    This can be a rubber thumb or piece of balloon.

Step 4

Knot will form here

Step 5

Top
Batting
Back

Step 6

Top
Batting
Back

the needle. Make the stitches as small as possible without worrying too much about the length. As you are quilting, make certain you clip your basting stitches so you do not quilt over them. It will take about three hours of *continual* quilting to break through what we call "the quilting barrier." At this point, the stitching will become even smaller, less of a conscious effort and more of a pleasure. It is important to stick with it and try to relax to avoid getting a pain in your upper back and neck area. ✷ *Helpful hint:* In order to keep eyestrain to a minimum, raise your eyes and look away from your work at least once every fifteen minutes.

10. When there is about 5″ of thread left on the needle, take a small backstitch, bringing the needle through the loop which is formed. Now, pull the thread tight to create a knot.

11. Stick the needle into the same hole as the knot, going down into the batting layer, and give a little tug to pop the knot down. Come up to the top approximately 1/2″ away. Take another very small backstitch and stick the needle down again; this time, come up 1/4″ away and cut the thread off.

The No-Knot Method

1. Cut a length of quilting thread approximately 36″ long.

2. Thread the needle, using a needle threader if necessary.

3. Stick the needle up through the three layers and pull up only half of the thread. Leave the other half hanging. You will work with only one half at a time.

4. Take a small backstitch and continue with the quilting stitches as described above. End as in Steps 10 and 11 of "The Knot Method" above.

5. Return to your starting point and thread the tail which was left hanging. Take a small backstitch and continue with the quilting stitches in the opposite direction, ending as above. If you are using a hoop, reposition it as necessary.

Most beginning quilters have a tendency to quilt around small shapes, one at a time. It is, however, faster and more efficient to quilt in one direction with long continuous lines.

With the quilting thread, measure along the line you wish to quilt, add 4″ to the measurement and cut the thread. This will ensure that you will not run out of thread halfway along the stitching line. Your stitches will be easier to make if you stitch toward yourself and then turn or angle toward the left-hand side (reverse for left-handed people). When you reach a seam intersection, slip the needle and thread under and beyond the seam allowances, into the batting layer, and bring the needle up at the next area to be quilted. Most intersections have thick seams which cause you to lose the rhythmic motion of the running stitches. You may need to take one or two stabs to get beyond the bulky seams. Then continue with the running stitch. If you are quilting a design with lines in two directions, or crossed directions, it will be helpful to thread two needles, working in one direction with one needle and in the opposite direction with the other needle.

Many people quilt 1/8″ to 1/4″ away from each seam line. This forms an indentation on each side of the seam, raising the stitched seam. It will also strengthen the seam line and give durability to your quilt. It will be

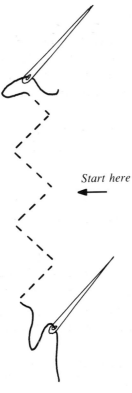

Start here

Steps 3-5

difficult to stitch closer than 1/4″ on the side to which the seam allowance has been pressed, as there will be two additional layers of fabric to stitch through.

✳ *Helpful hint:* If you are quilting in a hoop and have finished quilting for the day, remove the quilt from the hoop to avoid getting deep creases in it.

When you are done quilting, you are ready to turn to Chapter 10 for instructions on attaching the binding.

MACHINE QUILTING

SUPPLIES:
Sewing machine
Even-feed walking foot
An accessory foot to your sewing machine. It allows the three layers to feed evenly through the machine without puckering.
Sewing machine needle, #12 (#80)
Thread
In the bobbin, cotton/polyester to match the backing; cotton/polyester or nylon filament thread on the top. Smoky nylon thread is good when you have used many different colors in your quilt, because it will not show. We have, however, found that when nylon thread is used on quilts which will be washed, the cut ends of the thread can become sharp and sometimes the stitching lines will pop. For these reasons, nylon filament thread is not the best choice for utilitarian quilts. It would, however, be suitable for a wall hanging. ⊡ *Warning:* Unless you are experienced in working with it, do not attempt to machine quilt with nylon filament thread.

Steps 4-5

Machine quilting has gained popularity within the last few years. It is an excellent way to give design and texture to a quilt without devoting the many hours required for hand quilting. Machine quilting does not have to be limited to straight-line stitching. We recommend, however, that you try to tackle the more involved quilting patterns only after practice.

To machine quilt:

1. Attach an even-feed walking foot to your sewing machine. ✳ *Helpful hint:* To prevent the thread from puckering or your quilt from not feeding evenly through the machine, check to see that the walking foot is fitted on the machine properly, with the bar resting on top of the needle bar of the machine.

2. Adjust the stitch length to 8 to 10 stitches per inch. ✳ *Helpful hint:* Start with a full bobbin of thread. It is frustrating to run out of thread in the middle of a stitching line.

3. Now, lay the quilt out on a flat surface.

4. You will begin stitching near the center, preferably on a seam line. Roll two opposite sides of the quilt toward the center, leaving the seam or stitching area exposed.

5. Starting from the bottom, roll the quilt up toward the top.

6. Place the quilt into the sewing machine and stitch along the center line or area to be quilted, unrolling the length of the quilt as you go. ⊡ *Warning:* Be careful that this roll does not get caught up on your sewing table, preventing the quilt from feeding evenly through the machine.

7. Unroll the quilt, re-roll it and fold it to expose another area to be quilted. Continue until the entire quilt has been stitched. It is best to stitch all areas in one direction and then turn the quilt and stitch perpendicular to the first stitching lines.

8. Remove the safety pins.

You are ready to turn to Chapter 10 for instructions on attaching the binding to your quilt.

TYING

SUPPLIES:
#1 cotton darning needle
Perle cotton thread
Scissors

At this point your quilt should be layered, on a flat surface or in a frame, ready to be tied.

TYING WITH THREAD

To tie with thread:

For best results, place your ties no more than 6″ apart.

1. Thread the darning needle with a double thickness length of perle cotton (cut about a 60″ length of thread). Do not knot the end.

2. Choose a point in the center of the quilt where you would like to make a tie. Poke the needle down through all thicknesses and come up approximately 1/8″ away.

3. Move to the next spot to be tied and take a small stitch.

4. Working in one direction, continue across the quilt until you have run out of thread. You will want to take the stitches all in one direction.

5. Re-thread the needle and continue stitching until the entire quilt top is done.

6. With scissors, clip the threads between the stitches.

7. Tie a square knot at each point.

8. Trim off any excess thread if the tails are too long.

Proceed to Chapter 10 for instructions on attaching the binding.

TYING WITH RIBBON

SUPPLIES:
**Ribbon (either grosgrain or satin,
  1/4″ to 1/2″ wide)**
**Thread (cotton or cotton/polyester
  in a color to match the bows)**
Small scissors
Sewing machine
Pins

You may wish to secure the quilt with ribbon bows rather than ties.

To tie with ribbon:

1. Cut the ribbon into 6″ lengths.

2. Tie the ribbon lengths into bows.

3. Position the bows around the quilt and secure them in place with straight pins.

4. Take the quilt to the sewing machine. Because you want to begin stitching in place without any movement, set your stitch length and stitch width on 0. Place a quilt portion with the bow attached underneath the foot.

5. Remove the pin. Take a few stitches in place to secure the bow to the quilt. With the needle in the up position, move the stitch width to a wide zigzag. Take four or five stitches. Return the stitch width to 0 and take a few stitches to lock in the zigzag. Remove the quilt from the machine. Cut off the tails of the thread.

6. Repeat for the remaining bows.

Proceed to Chapter 10 for instructions on attaching the binding.

BINDING

SUPPLIES:
Sewing machine
Hand-sewing needle
Cotton thread
Glass-head pins
Plastic right-angle triangle
Steam iron
Pressing surface
Light-colored towel
Wide plastic ruler
Cutting board
Rotary cutter or fabric scissors
Plastic or metal tape measure

 The final step in completing your quilt is the application of a binding. A binding is a narrow strip of fabric that is used as a finishing edge over the raw edges of the entire quilt, encasing its three layers. The edges of the quilt receive a lot of wear and tear; you might notice, in looking at older quilts, that the edge is usually the first part to wear out. Although there are several methods of binding a quilt, we like the method described below because it is quite durable and will give longer wear to your quilt; it involves wrapping *two* layers of fabric around the edge of your quilt.

PREPARING YOUR QUILT FOR BINDING

Many times, after your quilt has been quilted, either by hand or machine, it may no longer be square. The stitching lines may have stretched it a little out of shape. This occurs generally along the edges and in the corners. Now is the time to straighten it up.

1. Lay the quilt out on a flat surface, top side up.

2. Place pins perpendicular to the edge every 3″ through all layers to hold it flat. This step will also prevent any chance of the backing being cut too small.

3. Use your wide plastic ruler to straighten the edges and, with the rotary cutter, remove any excess batting and backing. Use your plastic triangle to make sure the corners are at right angles. While you have the quilt flat, measure all four sides. Make a note of these measurements as you will need them later in "How to Determine the Length of Binding Strips."

BINDING YOUR QUILT

Binding strips can be cut on either the straight grain or the bias. Strips cut on the straight grain are easier to cut. Using them, a beginning quilter can easily achieve a finished edge without ripples. Left-over lengths of border or backing fabric can be used. Straight binding, however, is not appropriate for quilts which have curved or zigzag edges.

A bias binding requires more care. It is important to sew slowly and *not* stretch the binding (to avoid rippled edges). An even-feed walking foot will be helpful. Bias binding is a must for quilts with curved or zigzag edges.

CHOOSING THE WIDTH OF YOUR BINDING STRIPS

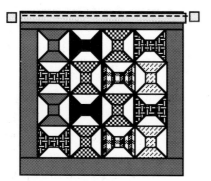

The cut width of the fabric strips you will be using for straight or bias bindings is determined by the finished width of the binding. We prefer a very narrow (1/4″) finished binding on quilts which have thin, flat batting, whereas a wider (1/2″) finished binding is easier to handle on quilts with thicker battings.

For a 1/4″ finished binding, cut strips of fabric 1¾″ wide.

For a 1/2″ finished binding, cut strips of fabric 3¼″ wide.

✱ *Helpful hint:* To cut bias strips, fold your fabric to form a 45-degree angle and cut.

HOW TO DETERMINE THE LENGTH OF BINDING STRIPS

To determine the cut length of straight binding strips, use the measurements from Step 3 above. Take an average of two opposite side measurements. Now add 2″ and cut two strips this length. Repeat this process for the other two sides of your quilt.

For a continuous bias binding, you must sew enough strips end-to-end to extend around the entire edge of the quilt. Add a 12″ working allowance.

ATTACHING BINDING STRIPS TO YOUR QUILT

To secure the layers of your quilt, use glass-head pins around its edge. Now, baste around the quilt, 1/8″ from the outer edge, by machine or hand.

Attaching a Straight Binding

1. Take one binding strip and fold it in half lengthwise, with the right side of the fabric on the outside. Mark the center point of the strip with a pin. Place a pin at the center point on an appropriate side of the quilt. Lay the binding strip on top of the quilt, lining up the raw edges of the binding strip with the raw edge of the quilt. Pin the binding strip to the

Step 2

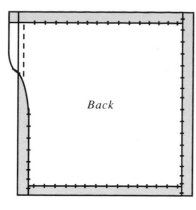

Steps 7-8

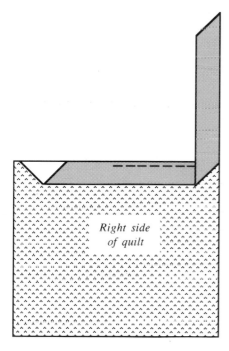

Steps 2-3

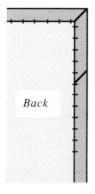

Step 5

quilt, matching up the center points and having 1″ of binding strip extend beyond the edge of the quilt at each end.

2. With the binding strip on the top, stitch through all thicknesses, from end to end, using a 1/4″ (for narrow binding) or 1/2″ (for wide binding) seam allowance. Ease in any fullness by pulling the binding taut while sewing. Trim off the excess 1″ from each end.

3. Fold the binding strip to the back side of the quilt and hand stitch it in place to the backing, using a small slip stitch.

4. Repeat this procedure for the opposite side of the quilt.

5. Next, attach the binding strips to the two remaining sides of the quilt, using the same technique except *do not cut* the excess 1″ from the edges of the binding strips. This excess is used to finish off the corners.

6. Flip the binding over the seam, then fold the 1″ excess under the quilt.

7. Hold the fold in place and fold the binding strip to the back side of the quilt. Pin along the length of the strip. Now, hand stitch it in place to the backing, using a small slip stitch.

8. Repeat Steps 6 and 7 for each corner.

Attaching a Continuous Bias Binding

You can begin binding anywhere along the edge of the quilt except in a corner. ✴ *Helpful hint:* After you have selected a starting point, run the binding strip around the edge of the quilt to make certain that a seam does not fall into a corner. If it does, readjust your starting point.

1. Fold your bias strip in half lengthwise, right side out. Line up the raw edge of the strip with the raw edge of the quilt top.

2. Leaving a 4″ tail, stitch the binding to the quilt with a 1/4″ (for narrow binding) or 1/2″ (for wide binding) seam allowance. Stitch up to the seam line in the corner. Take a few backstitches. Remove the quilt from your sewing machine.

3. Diagonally fold the binding strip away from the quilt.

4. Fold the binding straight down, even with the edge of the quilt. Stitch. Continue and finish all sides and corners in the same manner. When you are within 8″ of your starting point, remove the quilt from your machine. Adjust the two tails to fit together. Sew them to each other diagonally. Now, sew this joined strip of binding to your quilt.

5. Fold the binding to the wrong side and hand slip stitch it to the backing, stitching to the seam line in a corner. At the corner, fold the binding to form a miter. Continue stitching around the quilt, folding the remaining corners in the same manner. ✴ *Helpful hint:* This technique of mitering the corners can also be used on straight grain bindings.

Congratulations! You have successfully completed your quilt.

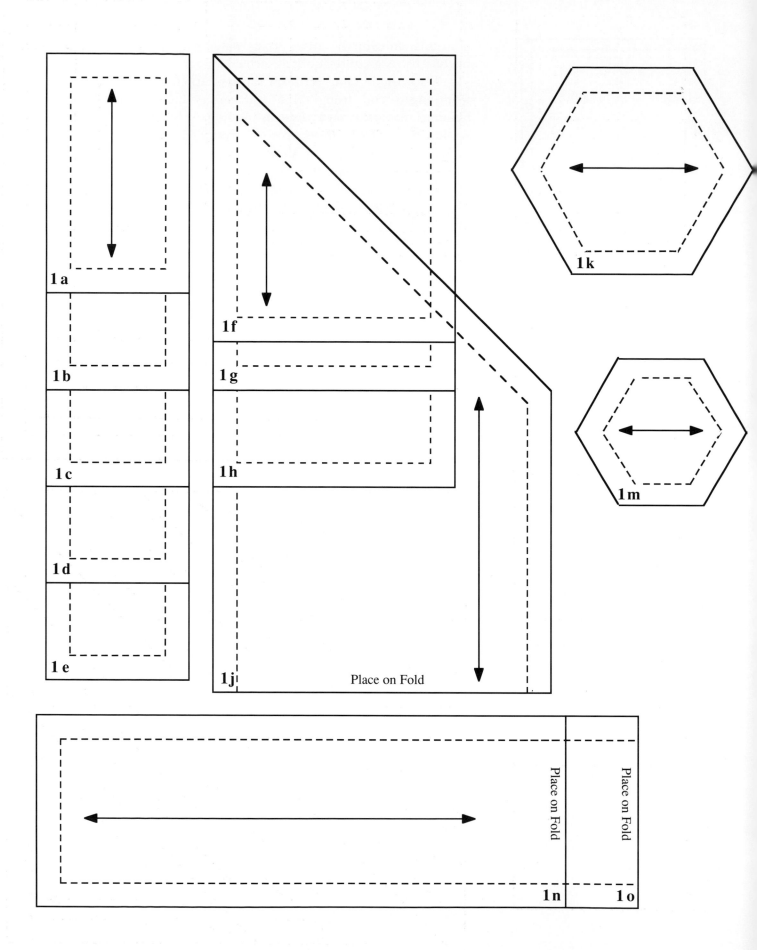

1a

1b

1c

1d

1e

1f

1g

1h

1j

Place on Fold

1k

1m

Place on Fold

Place on Fold

1n

1o

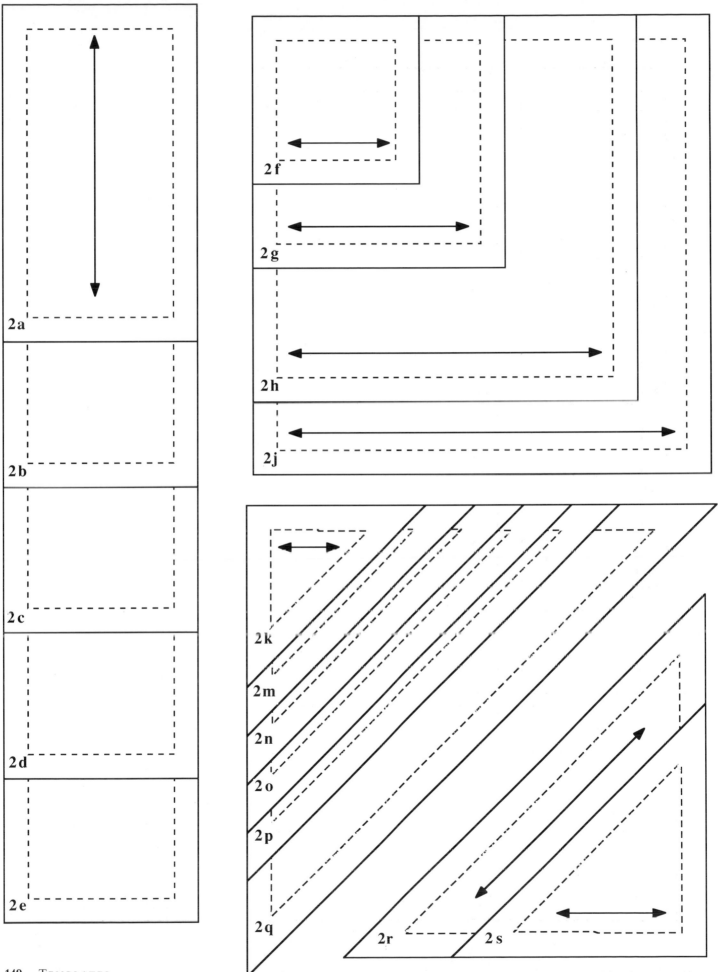

2a

2b

2c

2d

2e

2f

2g

2h

2j

2k

2m

2n

2o

2p

2q

2r

2s

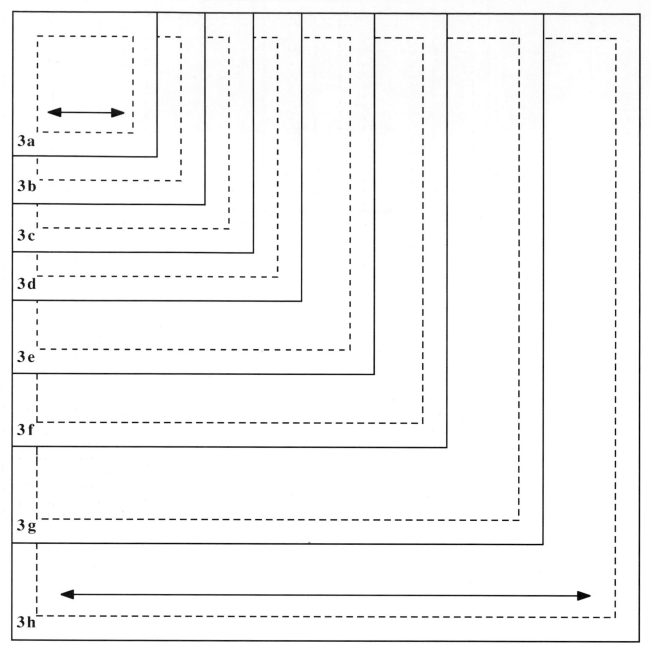

3a

3b

3c

3d

3e

3f

3g

3h

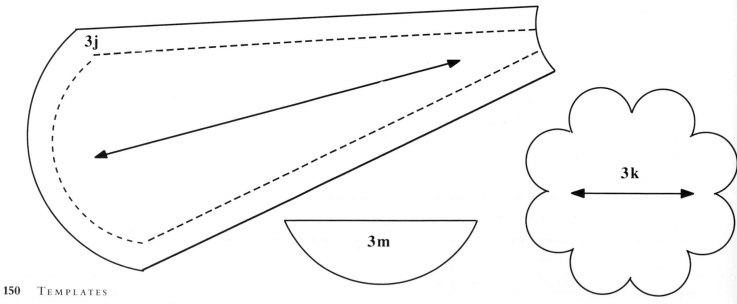

3j

3m

3k

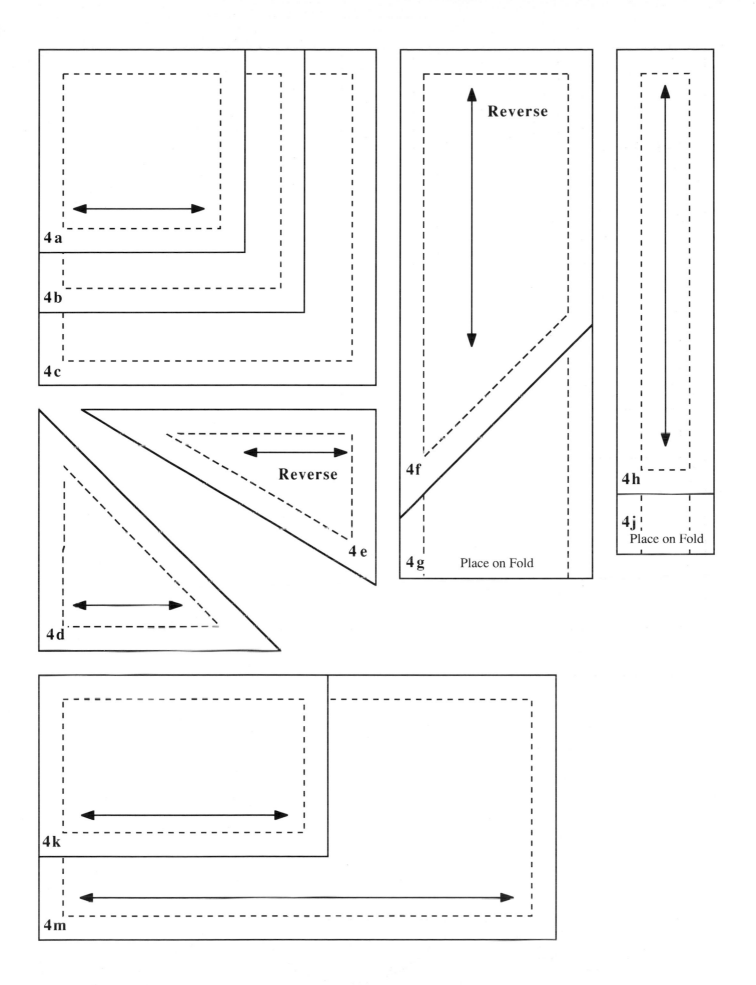

4 a

4 b

4 c

Reverse

4 f

4 g

Place on Fold

4 h

4 j

Place on Fold

4 d

Reverse

4 e

4 k

4 m

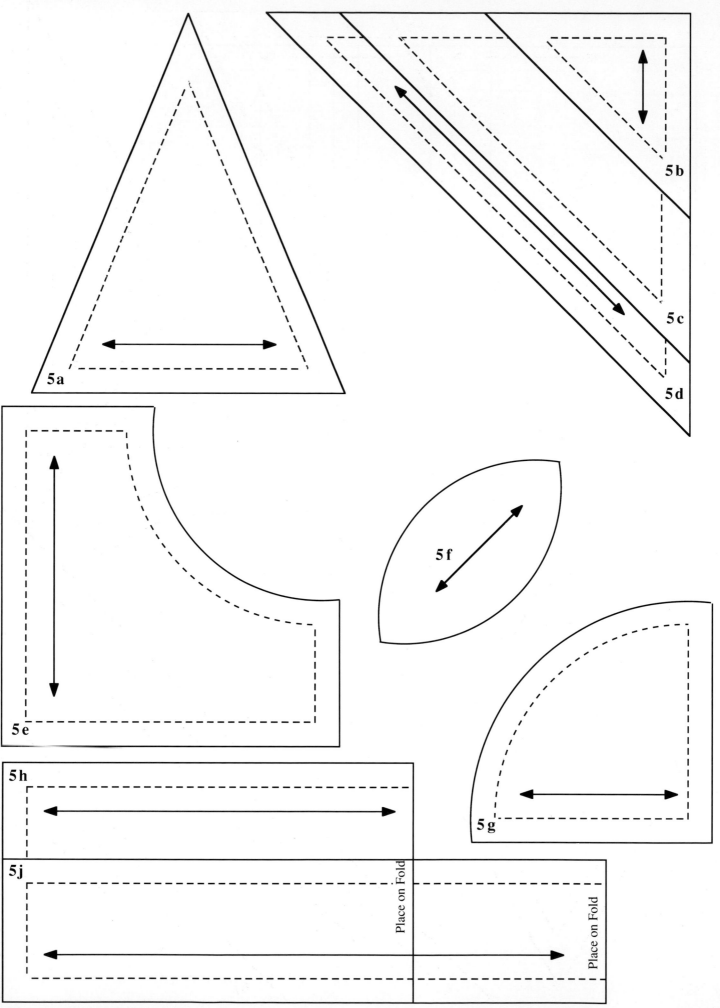

5a

5b

5c

5d

5e

5f

5g

5h

5j

Place on Fold

Place on Fold

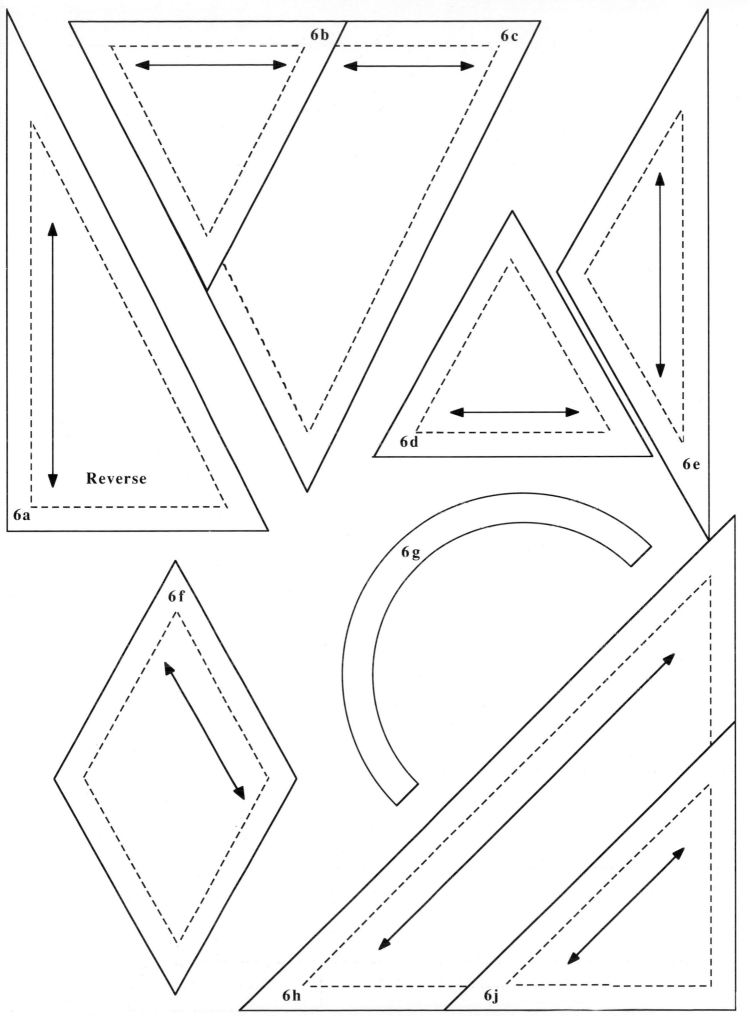

6b

6c

Reverse

6a

6d

6e

6g

6f

6h

6j

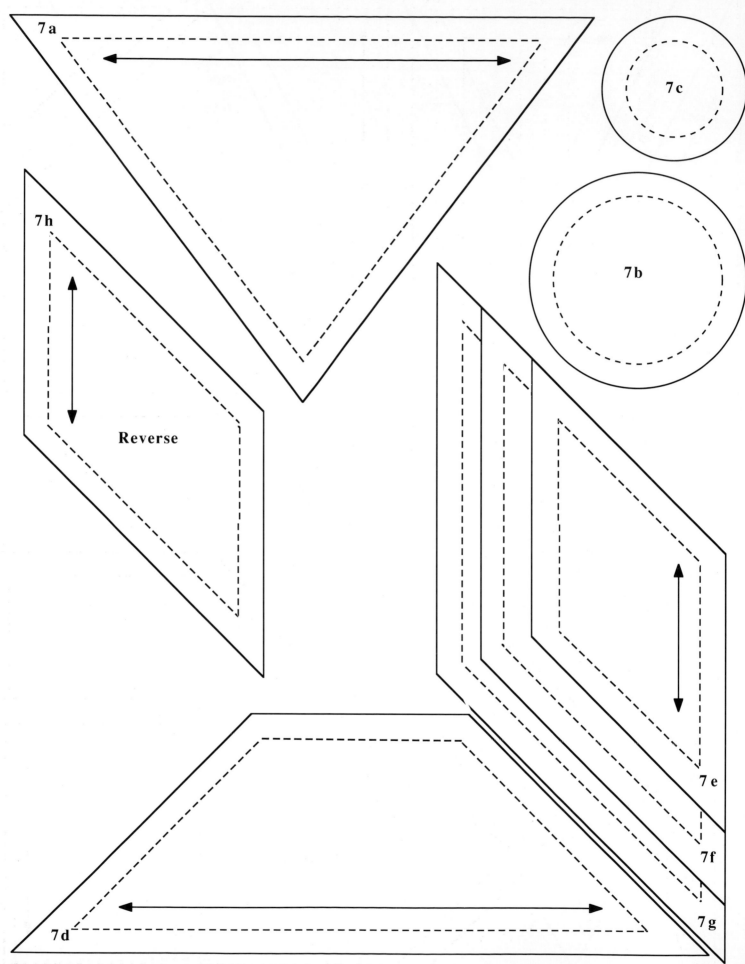

7 a

7 c

7 b

7 h

Reverse

7 e

7 f

7 d

7 g

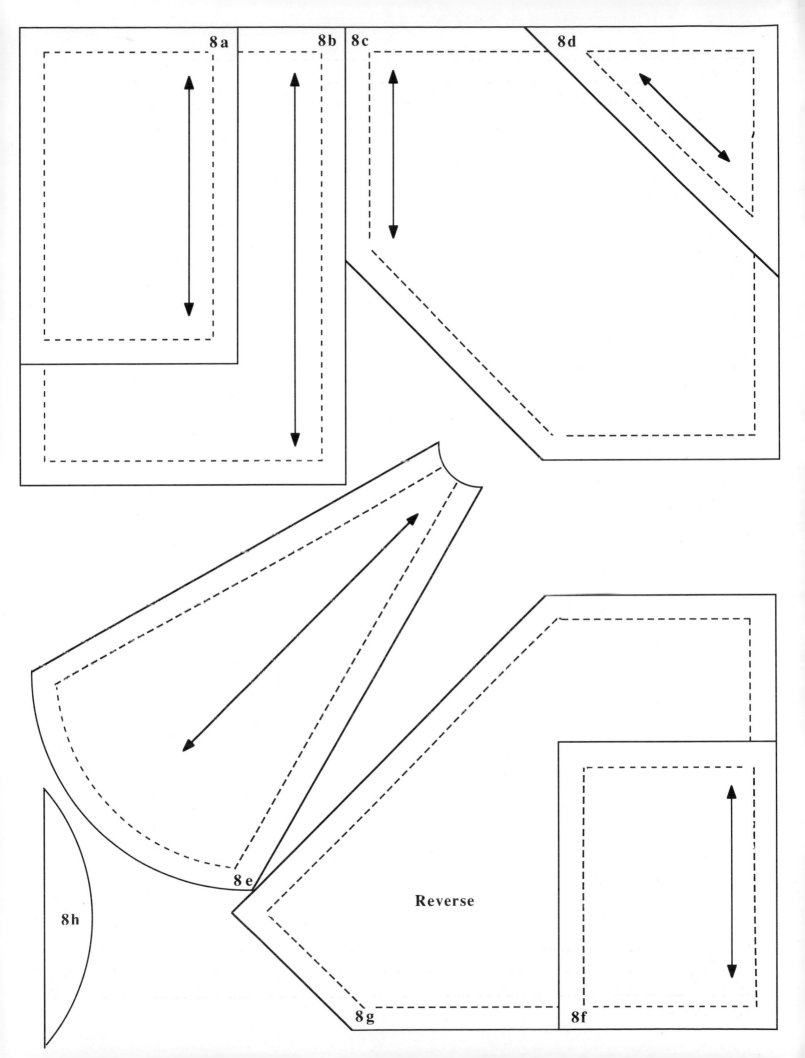

1/4 *Benicia Rose* block

HOW TO MAKE YOUR OWN
SCRAP SAMPLER QUILT

A twelve-week course using the scrap Sampler *quilt shown on page 9 on the nursery wall.*

Here is a twelve-week classroom schedule which we have found through experience works very successfully at teaching novices the basics of quiltmaking. The classes cover techniques essential to quiltmaking, from start to finish, in an organized, progressive sequence: the students receive a sampling of all techniques—quick, traditional, hand and machine piecing and hand quilting. The homework assignments will not overwhelm the students who are equipped with this book as their aid, and the assignments will prepare the students for class and therefore facilitate the flow of the classes. Because of the innate flexibility of this suggested outline, instructors can shorten or lengthen the course, even up to as much as twenty-four weeks.

Twelve 3-hour classes

CLASS ONE

Subjects: Thoughts on quiltmaking by instructor; anatomy of a quilt; understanding fabric; choosing a color scheme; supplies and equipment.
Demonstration: Cutting tools; sew order of *Fence Rail* block; pressing.
Student participation: Cut strips for *Fence Rail* block.
Homework: Construct *Fence Rail* block. Read Chapters 1, 2, 3 and 4 and instructions for *Log Cabin* and *Nine Patch* blocks in Chapter 2 and strip piecing techniques in Chapter 5. Choose fabrics for one 12″ *Log Cabin* block and four 6″ *Nine Patch* blocks.

CLASS TWO

Demonstration: Quick and traditional methods of cutting and piecing *Log Cabin* and *Nine Patch* blocks; hand and machine piecing techniques.
Student participation: Cut strips for *Log Cabin* and *Nine Patch* blocks. Construct *Log Cabin* block in class.
Homework: Construct four 6″ *Nine Patch* blocks. Read instructions in Chapter 2 and choose fabrics for one 12″ *Madison House* block.

SUPPLIES:
This book
1/4 yd. each of six 100% cotton fabrics graduated from light to dark
Cutting board
Wide plastic ruler
Rotary cutter
Notebook
Pencil

SUPPLIES:
Cutting board
Wide plastic ruler
Rotary cutter or fabric scissors
Neutral color cotton thread
For machine piecing: **Sewing machine**
For hand piecing: **#9 or #10 Between needle, small scissors, glass-head pins**
Fabric for *Log Cabin* and *Nine Patch* blocks

SUPPLIES:
Fabric for *Madison House* block
Cutting board
Wide plastic ruler
Rotary cutter
Glass-head pins
Thread
Sewing machine or hand sewing
    needle
Small scissors

SUPPLIES:
Fabric for *Heart* and *Postage Stamp
    Baskets*
Traced patterns
Thread to match heart and handle
    fabrics
Needle, #10 Between
Pencil
Sequin pins
Paper scissors
Fabric scissors

SUPPLIES:
Fabric for 12″ *Pine Tree* block
Supplies listed on page 103
    (substituting *Pine Tree* fabric for
    Pinwheel fabric) and on page 110
    for making templates

SUPPLIES:
Same as for Class Two and half-
    square triangles for both blocks

SUPPLIES:
Same as for Class Two and cut
    fabrics for one 12″ *Wild Goose
    Chase* variation and eight 6″
    Sawtooth Star blocks

CLASS THREE

Demonstration: Sew order for *Madison House* block.
Student participation: Cut fabric and construct *Madison House* block in class.
Homework: Read instructions in Chapter 2 and choose fabrics for four 6″ *Heart* blocks and one 12″ *Postage Stamp Baskets* block. Cut the background fabrics for all the blocks and trace four hearts and four basket handles onto plain paper.

CLASS FOUR

Demonstration: Paper-basting method of appliqué, back whipstitch, sew order for *Postage Stamp Baskets* block.
Student participation: Paper baste hearts and handles to background fabrics. Begin hand stitching shapes to background fabrics.
Homework: Complete any unfinished appliqué. Keep the four basket units separate as they will be used in the border. Read instructions for 12″ *Pine Tree* block in Chapter 2 and choose fabrics. Read instructions for half-square triangles, drafting, making, marking and cutting templates in Chapter 5.

CLASS FIVE

Demonstration: Making half-square triangles on the sewing machine. Drafting and making templates for the *Pine Tree* block; cutting fabric from the plastic templates. Sew order for the *Pine Tree* block.
Student participation: Draft, make templates for and construct the *Pine Tree* block.
Homework: Read instructions for *Bear's Paw* and *T Blocks* in Chapter 2. Choose fabrics for one 12″ *Bear's Paw* and one 12″ *T Blocks* block. Make the half-square triangles required for both blocks.

CLASS SIX

Demonstration: Sew order for *Bear's Paw* and *T Blocks* blocks
Student participation: Construct blocks in class.
Homework: Complete any unfinished blocks. Read instructions for double half-square triangles in Chapter 5. Choose and cut fabrics for *Wild Goose Chase* variation block according to the practice exercise on page 105. Choose and cut fabrics for eight 6″ *Sawtooth Star* blocks according to the instructions in Chapter 2.

CLASS SEVEN

Demonstration: Double half-square triangles. Sew order for *Wild Goose Chase* variation and *Sawtooth Star* blocks.
Student participation: Make double half-square triangles for all blocks and construct one *Wild Goose Chase* and two *Sawtooth Star* blocks. Do not connect the four units in one of the star blocks or in the *Wild Goose Chase* block, as they will be used separately in the border.
Homework: Complete any unfinished blocks. Read practice exercise for *Drunkard's Path* block and choose fabrics. Mark and cut templates from template plastic. Read instructions in Chapter 2 for *Kaleidoscope* block.

SUPPLIES:
Templates for *Drunkard's Path* block
All supplies listed in practice
    exercise for the block

CLASS EIGHT

Demonstration: Hand-piecing construction of *Drunkard's Path* block. Sew order for *Kaleidoscope* block.

Student participation: Begin hand piecing *Drunkard's Path* block. Draft and make templates for 6" *Kaleidoscope* block.

Homework: Complete the *Drunkard's Path* block. Construct four *Kaleidoscope* blocks. Keep the four blocks separate, as they will be used in the border. Read the instructions in Chapter 2 for one 12" *Attic Windows* and four 6" *Spool* blocks. Choose fabrics and cut strips for both blocks.

SUPPLIES:
Fabric strips for *Attic Windows* and
    Spool blocks
Template plastic
Permanent marking pens
Ruler with 45-degree angle
Graph paper
Large C-Thru ruler
Drafting tape
Paper scissors or rotary cutter
Cutting board
Wide plastic ruler
Glass-head pins

CLASS NINE

Demonstration: Drafting and cutting templates for *Attic Windows* and *Spool* blocks.

Student participation: Draft and make templates for *Attic Windows* and *Spool* blocks. Use templates to obtain the correct length and angle on the pre-cut strips. Begin constructing the blocks.

Homework: Complete *Attic Windows* and *Spool* blocks, if necessary. Do practice exercises in drafting *54-40 or Fight* and *Le Moyne Star*. Read Chapters 6 and 7; experiment with different settings on your design wall.

SUPPLIES:
All completed blocks
Reducing glass
Paper
Pencil
Marking pencils for hand quilting

CLASS TEN

Demonstration: Sew order for setting blocks together. Attaching mitered borders. Marking the quilting lines. Preparation of backing.

Student participation: Decide on a setting for blocks and make a diagram on paper. Select fabric for the border. Decide on quilting designs.

Homework: Sew blocks together. Attach border(s). Prepare backing fabric. Mark quilting lines, if needed. Read Chapter 8.

SUPPLIES:
Completed quilt top
Backing fabric
Masking tape
Cotton darning needle, #1
Cotton thread
Glass-head pins
Scissors

CLASS ELEVEN

Demonstration: Types of battings.

Student participation: Students break up into small groups and help baste each other's quilts.

Homework: Read Chapter 9.

SUPPLIES:
Basted quilt
Quilting hoop
Needle, #9, #10 or #12 Between
Quilting thread
Thimble

CLASS TWELVE

Demonstration: Quilting frames and hoops. The quilting stitch.

Student participation: Begin hand quilting in a hoop.

Homework: Continue quilting the quilt. Read Chapter 10.

Approximately six weeks later (after the students have had a chance to work with their hand quilting techniques), we get together, share thoughts and demonstrate attaching the binding.

We have found the reunion to be a great incentive for students to continue working on their quilts. They all love showing off their work and sharing their thoughts about the quilting experience.